Cracked Shell Whole Yolk

A Memoir

MARGO VIOLA

AuthorHouse™ LLC
1663 Liberty Drive
Bloomington, IN 47403
www.authorhouse.com
Phone: 1-800-839-8640

Author's note: This book is non-fictional. Each character is a real individual and each event is described as it occurred, or were related to me by others. All of the names of these said individuals and locations have been changed to protect their right to privacy.

Cover image by Brand X Pictures / Getty Images

Edited by Mary Linn Roby

Published by AuthorHouse 03/28/2014

ISBN: 978-1-4918-6115-8 (sc)
ISBN: 978-1-4918-6114-1 (hc)
ISBN: 978-1-4918-6113-4 (e)

Library of Congress Control Number: 2014902088

This book is printed on acid-free paper.

CONTENTS

ACKNOWLEDGMENTS

FIRST AND FOREMOST, I WOULD like to thank my creator and all of his ministering angels that wrapped their protective arms around me throughout all of my struggles and hardships.

Here is a special thank you to all my family members, beginning with my deceased mother. Mother I love you and I often feel you smiling down on me. To my daughter and grandson, you have been my fuel for motivation for many years. I love you both. To my stepfather, thank you for all of your unwavering support. To my husband, whom I love beyond words, thank you for your pure love. To my former husband, thank you for giving me a new identity to avert danger. I truly appreciate our relationship and all of the lessons it taught us. To my family members who suffered greatly and supported me through every ordeal and event, I love you all. To my deceased father, I am grateful for the lessons we taught one another, and for the forgiveness and closure I have obtained.

Many thanks would not be enough to show my gratitude for all the selfless acts of kindness shown by so many individuals. I wish to extend an extra special heartfelt thank you to all of my "warriors" who fought the great fight, with me, each and every one of you are uniquely amazing. You all have an honorary mention in this book because you are etched upon my heart for your good works and kindness. For privacy purposes you each are mentioned using first names only: Michelle, Sam, Jeffrey, Kyle, Bob, Barbara, Nancy, Melissa, Pat, Rabbi J, Jody, Doreen, Rus, Harriet, Steve, Mike, Cheryl, Kathy, Marco, Barbara, Nick, Ant, Joanne, Dennis, Catherine, Jen and Stacey. Each and every one of you, and others too numerous to mention, motivated me to write my life story.

Prologue: The Birth of a Book

Margo's journey began in 2008 when she and Vito embarked on a life-long journey in a marriage filled with love and adventure, during which they discovered both physical and spiritual harmony.

They began their lives together on a Norwegian ocean liner called *The Spirit* which departed from the New York harbor and headed for the Caribbean Sea, its tons of steel cutting through the Atlantic Ocean like a knife cuts through soft butter, sailing smoothly through calm waters, sparking with the dancing sunlight on a perfect sunny June day.

The couple sat on the balcony of their penthouse suite waiting for breakfast, intending to begin their honeymoon vacation with a breakfast toast. "To our life together, may it be a journey filled with love, compassion and tenderness, "Margo announced, to which Vito, tenderly touching her cheek, replied, "I've waited a lifetime to fall in love. You are my gift and I will cherish you and our love forever."

Later, the butler served a delicious breakfast of fresh tropical fruit, with a drizzle of dark chocolate syrup, layered over a chilled pool of vanilla yogurt while butter slid off the side of the whole grain pancakes and pooled on the edge of the plate. Coffee was accompanied by fresh cream and cubed sugar, and for extra protein, there were the hard-boiled eggs that Vito had requested. Holding one of them between his forefinger and thumb, he said, "Look babe, nature's most perfect food".

This was a classic jingle sung by Vito over the past couple of years whenever they ate eggs, whether they were prepared as egg white omelets, hard and soft-boiled eggs, or pouched and scrambled, just to name a few.

Since both of them were award-winning amateur bodybuilders, protein was an important part of their diets.

Now, on the first morning of their honeymoon, Margo cracked the shell of her hard-boiled egg and peeled the shell carefully to avoid chipping away at the layers of egg white. After a few divots into the white part of the egg, Margo pulls it back and reveals a yolk that was perfectly intact. It was, she thought, nature's most perfect analogy to life, to her own life to be exact. She had, like the egg's cracked shell, lived through years of dedicated effort to fight off the woes of her experience in order to emerge as a whole entity. How perfect her life was now that, for the past two years, she had experienced true love, whole and complete with the man of her dreams, that after nearly fifty years, she had been given the greatest gift of all, true love. It was a storybook beginning and she felt so blessed to be starting this fresh adventure, one filled with a wellspring of happiness and peace.

It was then that she knew that she must share her story with others, to inspire them to keep hope alive in their hearts, to tell them that she had once been a cracked shell who had faced adversity and now emerged as a whole yolk. And how better to begin than with her birth.

ONE

Family's Dynamics

My Story: Margo Viola

I was born the third out of four children, on April 21, 1961, and named Margo after my mother and grandmother. A lower middle-income family, my father a carpenter and my mother a homemaker, we lived in the inner city; Bronx, New York, also known as "South Bronx". According to my mother's account, I was such an easy baby to care for, docile and easy to please, that I had to be woken up to eat and to be changed. As my older brother and sister romped through the house, I sat by the sidelines, content to be a spectator despite the fact that my brother, a boy through and through, tried to get me to join in the family fun by pulling the wooden bars from the sides of the playpen. But I remained firmly grounded, exactly where our mother had placed me.

My mother was born in 1935, the first of five children. Her father was killed in the war while serving in the United States Army when she was only eight. As a result, being the oldest, she was responsible for her siblings and household chores, while her mother worked full time. This was a trying time for her, filled, as it was, with a tremendous amount of responsibility. A year or so later her mother remarried a man who would prove to be an abusive alcoholic, and it wasn't long before the abuse spread to her siblings, especially her two brothers. She tried to keep the peace in the home by doing chores, taking care of her brothers and sisters and keeping things light and calm which, although it worked sometimes, often proved futile. The violence continued in her home in spite of all her efforts.

It was in good part because of this that my mother escaped by marrying at sixteen to a man who, shortly after enlisted in the US Army and was sent out to war, only to return, eighteen months later as abusive an alcoholic as her stepfather had been in the home she had fled from. Her marriage consisted of drunken rages, physical altercations mixed with verbal abuse. Within sixteen months from the date of their marriage, the annulment process began, and she returned to her childhood home, labeled "Marked", "Used", "Divorcee" or "Easy". From that point onward, she bore the smudge of a failure, rejected and shunned by society.

It was no wonder that, after dating, for a short time, her best friend's older brother, she agreed to marry him, accepting his proposal as a way to flee from the house again. Jim Viola was well aware that Margo did not love him, but he told her that he hoped that, in time, she would. And although their marriage lasted for eighteen years, it did not have a storybook ending.

My father, Jim Viola, was born in 1932, the oldest of three children. His mother, a housewife, and his father, a hard worker and good provider, were old world of Italian decent. A very strict enforcer of the house rules, he was unwavering and uncompromising in his idea that a women's place was in the home, subservient to the man of the house, the king of the castle, and that children were to be seen and not heard. Husbands were meant to make a living, and should expect to have their meals ready when they returned from work, after which they often joined their friends, good ole boys, at the local tavern. In later years his drinking habits escalated, especially when my parent's marriage fell apart.

Growing up, I remember my mother being there for us at any time we needed her while my father watched television or slept in his favorite chair, snoring noisily. Our friends were not allowed to visit, and we had to play outdoor so as to not disturb him. My father wouldn't tolerate anything other than the set rules. If we acted up, he would pull out his belt from his pant loops and whip us. As for playing with us or helping with homework, my mother was expected to fulfill this role. As a result, I really didn't get to know my father as an individual, nor did I like him very much. It seems that the only time he had interaction with us was to reprimand or punish us. I kept to my mother's side most of the time. I was emotionally attached to her as well.

During the later years of my childhood, I remember that, since we were struggling financially on my father's salary, my mother expressed a desire to work-not that she didn't do the best with what she had. Many of our suppers consisted of hot dogs, beans or spaghetti with very little meat, and I remember her making homemade bread and soup made from left over vegetables mixed with flour. She also sewed clothing for us as well as drapes and painted rooms, covered old worn furniture, and hung wallpaper, to cover badly patched walls.

Facing the fact that our lack of money kept our family from living a better life, my mother often requested permission to work, a request my father, feeling insulted, always denied. My parents had many late night confrontations regarding the subject of my mother working, and because she never gave up, she was finally granted the right to work part time. This came, however, with the stipulation that her working hours did not interfere with the children's schedule, since she was expected to continue to perform her duties as both mother and wife, a proviso which resulted in her acquiring a night job at the Bronx Bank.

The year was 1969, a time of racial discord and upheaval; the inner city was unsettled in the South Bronx, to say the least. Our particular block, as they called them, consisted of families of Italian decent while houses on an adjacent street were owned by Black Americans. Racial tensions were so extreme that it was dangerous to leave our street without protection. The violence became so great that no one could walk the streets alone. A racial war between our two blocks was prompted, by one of the families on our street who sold their house to a Black American family.

As a result, the residents decided to obstruct each entrance of the street by sitting on beach chairs. The men instructed all of the women to gather the children and have a "sit in" at both ends of the block. For two days, the moving van could not break through the crowd of chairs until finally the police intervened by arriving with paddy wagons, and threatened to arrest everyone who was blocking the way. When everyone complied and removed the chairs from the middle of the street, a large moving van drove through very cautiously and parked in front of the row home about ten doors away from my own front door. By then it was almost dusk and the black family was fearful of moving their belongings into their new place after dark so the moving van remained parked in front of the property.

The Italian men that lived on our street had a secret meeting in one of our neighbor's kitchen and devised a plan to set the house on fire during the night. At around one in the morning, the house was an inferno. It burnt to the ground before the fire department was able to extinguish it. The next day I overheard my father talking to another dad on our block about how each man took a sledgehammer to the interior of that house before setting it ablaze. The smell of charred wood mixed with gasoline permeated the entire street. I can still feel the intense heat radiating from the pavement and buildings. I remember the police arriving to investigate the suspicious incident. When the police questioned many of the residence, including the children, to no avail, the fire was deemed "arson", set by an unknown individual or by individuals. No one spoke of that night ever again.

A time of uncertainty arrived at our home after that. Police barricades always appeared at the end of block during a racial riot which began with black men up on the rooftops across the street. Some had guns. Others had glass bottles they threw off the roof down unto the street below. My parents rushed us to our bedrooms which were located at the back of our house, that being the safest place for us to seek refuge, until the police riot team arrived dressed in full protective gear with bulletproof vests and Plexiglas shields, holding nightsticks and teargas canisters, along with rifles and other defense weapons. I could hear the mega phone echoing the authorities' demand for surrender as the situation rapidly defused. No deaths occurred but there were a few casualties resulting from violence which resembled a mini civil war. The police filled the vans with the lawbreakers, and exited the street quickly. Both sides were embittered with resentment and hatred for one another.

It was my mother's top priority was to remove her children from what she considered a war zone, and with that in mind, she worked all night to keep her job in order to save enough money to move us out of a city filled with turmoil. It was a great relief when we finally moved from our row home in the Bronx to a single-family home in the Greenwich, Connecticut suburbs.

At age ten, my life seems relatively positive. I lived in a nice house in a safe neighborhood. I attended private Catholic School where I acquired many new friends. Life was good for the next couple of years until one day, quite unexpectedly, that peacefulness came to an abrupt halt.

The illusion ended when I came home from school and witnessed my father leaving the house carrying two suitcases. It was an earth-shattering realization that my life was about to change. Pulling myself together as best as I could, I ran into my house to make sure my mother was still home, frightened that she might be next to leave. I was only ten years old. I could not absorb the magnitude of what was occurring. It would take tragedy and tremendous sorrow to finally arrive at an understanding of my family dynamics, dynamics that my mother had kept hidden from us children because, coming from a violent background herself, it was extremely important to her that there were no arguments or verbal confrontations in front of her children, always protesting when our father threatened to beat us. I know now that my parents must have ironed out all their disagreements at night, after we were fast asleep. With my father's departure, however, I lost my family, my security, and my reality. My idea of a family's core system was forever altered. That evening things grew worse. The events that took place that night would stay within me for an entire lifetime.

It was certainly a terrifying night to remember. As my father's car sped away, I ran back into the house to confirm that my mother was still there with us, and even though reassured that she was still there, I stood in the kitchen crying. My tears were not for the absence of my father, but for the instability of my world.

My mother, visibly upset, sat me down and attempted to explain just what was happening, although a full explanation of why it was happening would not come for quite some time. My head spun when she told me that she and my father were no longer in love with one another and that my father would be living somewhere else from that day forth. However, as she was preparing to go to work that evening, he suddenly appeared, intoxicated and extremely agitated. Blocking my mother from leaving the bedroom, he screamed obscenities at her and threatening her with bodily harm. This was not the father I had known my whole life. This man was and enraged lunatic.

Suddenly, without warning the bedroom door slammed shut, although we could still hear him shouting and her trying to reason with him. "I love you!" he yelled "Can't you see that, I love you so much I'll kill you! If I can't have you, I will make your face so ugly that nobody will want you!"

The silence that followed terrified me, and taking a heavy crystal bowl from the dining room table, I ran into the bedroom to find my father on the floor straddling my mother who appeared to be unconscious, her face bloodied. When I tried to reach her, and he pushed me away, I raised the bowl high and sent it crashing down on his head. For a moment he seemed dazed and then, stumbling to his feet, he pushed me into the hallway and fled the house like a wounded animal.

Crying uncontrollably, I ran to get ice and a towel, relieved that my mother had regained consciousness, although her face was badly marked up and extremely swollen and she was incapable of moving her right arm as well as experiencing intense pain from the shoulder. Insisting that I not call the police or medical emergency people, she told me that she was all right, and that I had to stay with my little sister, until my older siblings returned home, adding that she was going to get medical help for herself, and that she would come back for me later.

I followed her out to her car and as it backed away, ran after her, crying, "Please don't leave me here." But it was no use. I stood in the dark street and watched the car's brake lights until they became a dim red hue, my face moist with the salt from my tears. My body was limp with exhaustion, and my mind was racing with thoughts of fear and abandonment.

I went back to the house feelings alone and fearful of my father's return. After all I was the one who had hurt him in order to save my mother, the woman who had left me, the woman who had lied about always being here to protect us. Everything was wrong, and it must be my fault.

The result of that night would shape my concept of a family unit for a long time. My mother was treated for a broken cheekbone, a fractured arm and a dislocated shoulder, but the real long-term damage was the mental trauma she suffered, a trauma so severe that she did not return for six months, paralyzed with fear that our father might return to retaliate. During all of this, we children suffered tremendously.

As for my father, he had suffered a broken collarbone. According to this doctor, if he had been struck closer to the neck, there was a good chance the injury would have been fatal. As far as his mental capacity was concerned, he was in a bad state, falling into a deep depression. His alcohol consumption increased to outrageous proportions.

That evening was my introduction to abusive behavior, molding as it did my concept of family dynamics and relationships. Now my home environment was characterized by insecurity, sorrow and tragedy as everything took a turn for the worse.

The days and months following that tragic evening were filled with uncertainty. Many nights, my father came home late from the local taproom, usually in a drunken stupor. His moods were unpredictable. Some nights he wailed over having been abandoned by our mother. During his crying jags, he would tell us how much he loved her, while at other times he was jovial and would come home singing. His favorite song was, "You picked a bad time to leave me, Lucille. Four hungry children and a crop in the field . . ." On other nights he would wake up all of us and make us sit around the kitchen table, as he went on a rant in which he called our mother a whore and worse.

As I've said, my mother was absent from our lives for a period of six months during which I took on many responsibilities, cooking and cleaning, organizing my baby sister's uniform for school, making her lunches and helping her with her homework. My older sister and brother were out of the house most of the time, leaving my younger sister and me to fend for us. Often times, when we ran out of oil we would turn the electric stove on and leave the door open, in order to provide some heat. Food was limited and scarce. I remember making cinnamon toast by the stacks just to fill our empty stomachs. The telephone was turned off more often than turned on.

During this time, my sister Joan was being courted by a guy name Lee Chi, half Caucasian and half Asian, our next-door neighbor. Since he lived right next to us, Joan and he spent most of their time there. Joan told me they would stay up in his bedroom and smoke pot. They became inseparable, even though Joan often said that he was very controlling and that she was going to end their relationship.

However, when she tried, Lee became desperate and unreasonable. Once when she had left the house to meet her friends, she returned crying and rambling on and on about Lee threatening her. Suddenly, Lee appeared and chased her up to her bedroom. When she pleaded with him to stop hitting her, he accused her of having sex with her little brother. She was crying and screaming that he was crazy and when my older brother tried to protect her with a kitchen knife, he pulled a switchblade. Thankfully, neither of them suffered serious wounds. They called a truce, broke up and parted ways.

But that was not the last we heard of Lee. A few weeks later, Lee was knocking at our front door, asking for Joan who found herself having to sneak in and out of her own house, constantly feeling watched by Lee who, light on his feet, would often appear without warning, often at dusk. Lee would peer in the window next to the front door or follow her down the driveway, pleading with her to become his girlfriend again, which, after a while, she did.

Lee was not our only problem. We had our house broken into by some neighborhood troublemakers who smashed a window in the basement, and vandalized our property, by tossing everything upside down. They also spray painted a vulgar message on our basement wall, which read, "I want to fuck your oldest daughter." They even tried to steal our car but couldn't get it started. Instead, they pushed it down our driveway, crashing it into a concrete wall. I swore that it was Lee trying to scare my sister. The police took a full report but no one was ever charged with the crime. Even though the message referred to my older sister, it certainly scared me. I was afraid they would come get me too. Living without protection, I was left to ward off danger by myself, which was certainly scary enough. Many nights my little sister and I would huddle together in the living room floor for comfort, warmth and safety.

There was one evening when we both heard a noise and put our heads under the blankets, hoping that whoever was outside, would not find us there in the corner of the living room. It seemed like time was suspended. I counted the nothingness in the air, the safe sound of silence, as we remained curled together in a ball until Joan came home with Lee and another guy named Don. Lee and Don left Joan lying on the porch in a lounge chair in order to go down to the lake to smoke pot. As she told me later, a man wearing a black ski mask appeared, and standing on the side step, proceeded to masturbate. Thinking that Lee was playing a dirty trick on her, Joan jumped up from the chair, screaming at him, whereupon the man took off running through our yard into an open field next to our property.

Later that evening, when Lee returned and she told him what had happened, he didn't believe her, but when the fellow reappeared, still wearing his ski mask, Lee chased him and was stabbed in an artery in the thigh. Blood was everywhere when Joan helped him back to the porch and called for an ambulance. My younger sister and I watch, terrified, as the drama unfolded. When the police arrived, the detective in charge, a burly Italian, refused to believe Joan and Lee's story of the guy with a ski mask, convinced that it had been a domestic dispute even though the truth of the matter was that there was a crazy man loose in our town, and he remained at large and free to terrorize more innocent people.

Months later, Joan and Lee's relationship ended in trauma. Lee was so abusively jealous that Joan decided to break up with him for good. And because she was afraid of his reaction, after leaving him a note with the news, she took both my sister and me with her to walk to a relative's house where she would be safe, only to find that Lee was following us. When Joan told us to start running to get further away from him, I took hold of my little sister's hand and we began racing to safety. Cars whizzed by us, the wind from their vehicles brushing against our backs until we were forced to stop because my little sister's feet couldn't carry her any further.

We stood on the side of the highway watching Lee run past us and gain speed as he approached Joan and engaged her in conversation. And when she turned away, he took something shiny from his pocket, and raising it high over his head, plunged it into his abdomen. Later Joan explained that Lee had threatened to stab himself if she broke up with him but that she didn't really believe that he would do it. He was taken to a local hospital where he underwent counseling but, as far as Joan was concerned, this act sealed the fate in their relationship. Joan and Lee split for good without further incidents.

As the days forged forward, I grew increasingly angry about, my newly added responsibilities, and toward my parents for their role in a situation which left me feeling alone and unloved. I was filled with contempt for both of them for the roles they played, my father for hurting my mother and for chasing her away from us and also my mother for leaving me.

However, during these months, I attempted to live a normal life just like all of my schoolmates. I had been a catcher on my Catholic school softball team and I continued to attend practice sessions as if nothing bad was happening in my world. I no longer had transportation to and from after school activities and weekend games, so I rode my bike the four miles to the school field. I played each game with all my heart and soul. It was my escape from the reality at home. No one I knew ever came to watch or cheer or point or smile. But I was determined to blend in and have that short time of normalcy, in my life in spite of the craziness at home.

Six months elapsed before our mother returned to us. She came to visit while my father was at work. Thrilled to see her, I held on to every word she spoke. But my enthusiasm turned into dismay when I heard he tell us that she was preparing to have us live with her because "preparing" meant that it was not going to be today which left me filled with anger, disgust and hurt! At that point, six months seemed like a lifetime to me. Little did I know that I would live like that for an additional year before she was able to provide us with a home.

Eighteen months later, my mother returned for us, but my older brother and sister, set in their routines, refused to go with her. My father's brainwashing played a large role in their decision to stay with him. He had poisoned their minds, but my younger sister and I volunteered to move into our new environment in Stamford, Connecticut at once.

To my surprise, my mother had given birth to another child during her absence. Now, it seemed, we had a baby sister named Clara. I soon discovered that my mother had had a boyfriend prior to ending her eighteen-year marriage, and that with her biological clock ticking, they made the decision to conceive a child out of wedlock. My stepfather, Ed, was eleven years younger than my mother and had never been married before. He loved my mother and wanted them to marry and raise a family they could call their own. He had a full understanding of my mother's current marriage and the complications that were involved with it. He also realized that her age demanded that they conceive a child at once. The risk was far too great to wait for a full-fledged divorce decree. And even though this explained the months my mother was absent from our lives, I was left with a tremendous amount of mixed emotions. I felt relieved that she came back to get me, but I was hurt and angry for the pain I had suffered. I felt like an old toy, tossed aside, no longer fitting into my mother's new life, along with relief that she had finally returned to rescue me. In my heart I was willing to accept anything to be a part of a normal family.

At the last minute, my younger sister decided to stay living with our father but I didn't care. In my eyes, joining my new family was a fresh start. As far as I was concerned, it was a dream come true, and I was excited that, at last, I would be living in a warm and loving household, with my mother, my stepfather and a newborn baby who belonged to two people who were in love. All the ingredients for a fairy tale life were present, with the exception of the white picket fence. To me it appeared comparable to a Norman Rockwell poster.

But somehow I felt like an outsider, an observer in a house filled with happy people. I was twelve years old and hormonally unsound. I secretly viewed my stepfather and half-sister as the intruders who had replaced me and resented them accordingly. I felt that they were responsible for stealing my happiness, leaving me feeling that I was the intruder in this new world. I became convinced that, in order to be happy, I would have to make new friends.

TWO

Introduction To A New Relationship

WITH MY NEW HOME CAME a brand new school which was completely different from the Catholic school I had attended previously, complete with a homeroom that I reported to every morning. It was there that I met my first love, the person I would ultimately become attached to for the rest of my life.

On the first day, I found room 106 and sat down in the first available seat in the row next to the door, the third seat down. I felt uneasy as I looked around trying to gather my bearings, feeling very much a stranger when a small-framed girl with dark hair and nice warm smile introduced herself as Karin Manio. With a last name like that it was my guess that she was of Italian decent. Karin would become one of my very close friends in the years ahead.

Because Karin and I had many of the same classes together and shared the same lunch period, as well, my first day at my new school was turning out to be pretty promising. And since she had lived in Stamford, Connecticut all of her life, Karin helped me by introducing me to other kids my age.

The next day, as I reported to homeroom, my attention was drawn to a boy who sat across from me. Tall and slim with wavy dark hair, he had an attitude of a "Mr. Tough Guy," a cool, modern day James Dean, who, I later discovered, was named Sean Donnelly. And even though he didn't so much as a look my way, I instantly fell for him. When I leaned over and whispered something funny, he smirked and that was it for me; I could barely keep my heart from beating out of my chest. Here, I thought was the missing link to my happiness.

From that day forward, Sean was the focus of all my attention. I gravitated to his group of friends who were mostly older students in high school since he had this air of toughness about him that kept most of the other guys his age away. There was an unspoken fear of Sean which translated into respect, and I knew that I had to be a part of his life. Sean had taken hold of my heart; He was my world.

Before the month's end, Sean and I were a couple, spending all our breaks together. After school we went to his neighborhood hangouts where I got to know many of his friends and the girls they dated, including a couple named Cookie and Donny, Sean's closest friend who had dropped out of school a year earlier. Cookie's real name was Doris Campbell. She and I became very close. I hung out with her even when the guys were busy doing their own thing.

Engrossed in my new preoccupation, I moved further away from my family. Often I had my mother drop me off at Sean's development and frequently made plans for weekend sleepovers on many weekends at Cookies or my friend Karin's house. Karin came from a family of ten children so supervision was not a priority. As for Cookie, she lived with her younger brother and a divorced mother who was rarely home because she worked long hours. And since there was little or no supervision, Cookie's house was a teenager's dream hangout spot, a place where we were free to do whatever moved us, including drinking and smoking pot. We made all the wrong choices a teenager could make when left on their own. Finally, life was fun for me. It seems like my new life was taking shape. All my past memories of my parent's tragic divorce were light years away. Things seemed to be complete for me now that I found a new life with someone to love, and a lot of fun to be had. My biggest problem was figuring out how to get from my mother's house to Cookie's or Karin's.

Meanwhile, my relationship with Sean grew to a whole new level. I was so in love that I couldn't get enough of him. But when we became sexually involved, his attitude changed and he became increasingly possessive. At the time, I was flattered that Sean loved me enough to be jealous if I even talked to another boy. I believed that his behavior was a perfect way of showing me that he loved me, even though, because they were afraid of him, other guys began to avoid me.

Six months into our relationship, my life took yet another turn, one that turned out to be pivotal. One afternoon when we were walking to his house together, I noticed that he seemed agitated and nervous. For a while he said nothing but then, suddenly, began ranting on and on about a party we had attended at Roger's the previous week, while his parents were away, a party at which there was alcohol, marijuana and drugs in ample supply. When Sean accused me of having sex with Roger that night and I protested, he hauled off and punched me in the eye, knocking me to the ground. I cupped my face in hand as Sean continued to strike me about the head and back with his fist, and begged him to stop until finally I realized, when he began pulling me by my hair, that less resistance meant less pain. It wasn't until we approached a traffic light that Sean even notice that I was bleeding.

When Sean realized how hurt I was, his mood quickly changed from menacing to being concerned. And going on and on about how he hadn't meant to hurt me, he took me to his house and brought me ice wrapped in a towel to hold it to my eye. His sincere remorse left me desperately wanting to believe that this incident was a one-time event. And then his focus changed to how we were going to explain it, particularly to my parents at which point he proceeded to blame me for his decision to be punish me. Confused, I somehow found myself feeling guilty, as well as being overcome with the need to protect him and found myself soothing him and easing his mind by thinking of a story to tell my parents.

In the end, Sean was spared all consequences for his abusive behavior. Intent on covering the boy I loved, I told my parents that I had fallen off a horse. Ironically enough, the result was that, Sean vowed never to hit me where it would be visible. Now Sean favored hair pulling and shadow boxing me. There were times that he would make me stand in front of him and cover my face while he punched me. It was his way of humiliating me, and at the same time amusing him by demonstrating his physical prowess.

As we forged forward, the dynamics of our relationship became more complicated. The ingredients of Sean's background were a perfect mixture for the molding of an abusive offspring since he came from a family background filled with violence. The youngest of three children by eight years, he lived with an alcoholic father whose wife, Sean's mother, had left home, just as my mother had, and remarried.

I would wear the many battle scars that represented his mistrust and distain for women in general. Sean followed the example of his father who taught him to act out his anger by inflicting physical pain on others, wearing violence like a badge of honor; a badge that he shared with the man with whom he claimed to be "thicker than thieves."

Naturally, psychologically conditioning coupled with a violent living environment molded Sean's abusive behaviors. To him this was a completely normal way of life. His father, incapable of being a role model, became his "buddy," and many of the arguments between them became knock-down drag-out fistfights. Sean would steal his father's car and when the police got involved, look to his father to save him. Later the two of them would have a full-blown battle over Sean's behavior. They continued to live together like this for another twenty years until Sean's father had a stroke and was confined to a wheel chair.

It was during the tumultuous time when I fell in love with him that Sean began to use heroin and alcohol to numb the pain of his family life. His older brother, Hank, lived away at college where, perhaps because he was on the boxing team, he was often called upon to discipline Sean as he had done when, earlier, living at home. Now Hank was the good son, the son that attended college and was a star boxer while Sean was the son hooked on heroin and alcohol, the son who was suspended from school often enough to quit permanently, his only club the local police sweep.

As a result, the path Sean chose was one of destruction. His relationship with Hank went far beyond sibling rivalry. The two brothers were at war. In the end, Hank's method of controlling others led him to become a strong arm for the Bronx mobsters until he was caught by the F.B.I. He was later sentenced to a five-year term of imprisonment in Federal prison. His gladiator physique and mentality brought him many days of regret. And when he was released, there were many more years of physical altercations between the brothers.

After Sean's parents split up, his drug and alcohol use increased and he became even angrier and more violent toward anyone who was close to him. His sister Colleen, perhaps because she felt sorry for him, yet and was rarely home, was the one exception. She became the only maternal influence in his life, willing to bail him out of trouble, to keep the peace in the house. Sean would learn to play on her emotions in future years, verbally abusing her by calling her a slut and a whore whenever she denied a request, usually for money. Her method of controlling this sort of situation was to smooth it over. This usually was achieved by giving in to Sean's demands.

During a five year period, Sean and I broke up several times and each time we reconciled, his violence seemed to increase. He would describe how he was going to hurt me. He told me that my family members would be next, that he would hurt them. He would confirm my fear that if he couldn't get to me, he would certainly get to my loved ones. He followed me to my friend's houses. He stalked me at classmate's parties. And when some of the guys from school tried to stop him from forcing me to leave with him, Sean beat every one of them to a pulp with the result that I would go with him voluntarily when I knew an innocent person would be beaten because of me.

His violence seemed to know no limits. He dragged me off of high school grounds after my bus dropped me off, walking up behind me and whispering such threats in my ear I know that I had to go with him in order to avoid a scene at school. The few times that I refused, he dragged me off the school property, and soon I learned to appease him from the start. My goal was to make him happy and please him rather than infuriate him, although it seems that, as time passed, it became more difficult to satisfy Sean. He was so quick to anger. He would be completely fine one moment and a raging bull the next moment. I missed so many days of school in tenth grade that I had to go to summer school.

No one was exempt from Sean's rage. The list of people Sean physically assaulted ranged from neighborhood kids to family members. One day in particular, Sean attacked his mother and father when they tried to make him go to counseling for his drug and alcohol problem after he had been picked up several times by police. Once, after a fight in which his brother's jaw was broken, and Hank had to be taken to the hospital, Sean was taken to the Connecticut Psychiatric Hospital which was, essentially, a mental institution where he remained for a six-month period before he was released to the custody of his father.

It was during that time that I had the most empathy for Sean because of his letters which were filled with the pain of what he considered as being rejection by his parents. Clearly desperate to be loved, he wrote about how our love would blossom and grow. It was during this time that, once again, I wanted to love him, forgive him and, most of all, help him to change. I would prove my love for him by being there supportive and dependable. Sean would then trust in my love and me as a good person. He would clearly see that I was worthy of his love. He would plainly understand that I was one person in his world that would be there for him in rough times. His mind and heart would heal and love me back. That was my dream for us.

When Sean came home, we again resumed what I know now was a sick relationship. He became increasingly suspicious of everyone around us, showing definite signs of paranoia. He trusted "no one", especially women who would, he claimed, only betray him. He wore the diagnosis of "Borderline Personality Disorder" like a medal of honor. Our union fell deeper into the abyss of darkened and explosive misery.

Sean was verbally abusive as well as physically violent. There were rules of the relationship that I had to abide by. The main rule was that Sean ran the show. I was to obey his every whim. As a result, I became isolated in Sean's world, only associating with permissible people who included my own family and close friends. I was no longer permitted to speak with my close friend Karin who, Sean said, was a pig, claiming to have had sex with her. In Sean opinion I was enough of a slut on my own without extra outside influences like her. The only reason I was allowed to be around Cookie was because she was his best friend's broad, not because he had a good opinion of her character. There was no limit to his efforts to control me. He gave strict instructions about how I was to dress. There were specific guidelines that extended to the colors that could be worn, red being strictly forbidden. The consequences of breaking these rules and regulations would, he promised, be severe physical punishment.

Some of the punishment involved interrogation during sexual intercourse. A question from him would demand an answer no matter what we were doing. Although I always cooperated in an attempt to avoid confrontation, my response was never the right one. He would request certain sexual positions or make specific request for oral sex, and then when I did what he asked me to, he would call me a whore, slut or pig for knowing how to perform so well.

Sean was in complete control of me and the freedom of my thoughts and actions. Depending upon the infraction, he would sometimes hold me in a room for hours while he tortured me emotionally. Other times he burnt me on my forearms with a cigarette. He would make me lie face down on the floor next to the bed or sofa, telling me that I wasn't good enough to lie next to him, and threatening to hurt me if I move or ran away. More than once, he held a knife to my neck and threatened to cut my throat wide open. One constant refrain was that he would hurt my family if I ever left him. Sean watched me closely as he recited a long list of terrible things he suspected I had done. Some were just examples of my inadequacy as a human being. Other accusations reflected his imagination running a muck.

My only recourse in avoiding such physical altercations was to run off and so I became very skilled at sensing danger, although he hated the fact that I could predict his mood changes. He further despised the fact that I would run away from him as I sometimes did when I felt that I was in tremendous danger. There were situations that occurred in which, knowing that I might soon have to take cover, I would scan the room for the nearest exit. There were times that Sean would give me a head start, just so that he could chase me, catch me and then beat me up, right there where we stood. We would start out in Sean's family room. He would make me take off my shoes, open the sliding glass door and tell me to start running, and then at the count of five, run after me across the golf course on which many memorable beatings took place, not to mention threats of killing me in one of the more secluded sections. I believed Sean and feared him and his volatile moods.

And he was not the only one. Sean's best friend Donny also abused his girlfriend Cookie. She and I would take turns running from our boyfriends. We remained bonded together as close girlfriends primarily because we shared many of the same experiences and real fears. We always broke up with the guys at the same time. It was as if we fed off of one another's strengths, giving each other the courage to walk away from our torturers. Donny was a few years older than us. He had a driver's license and a truck in which he and Sean sometimes stalked Cookie and me.

Often times they would drive up to private parties at schoolmate's houses. One of them would jump out of the car, and in a menacing manner, demand that we get into the car with them, knowing that no one would dare object.

Sean enjoyed intimidating anyone that would look his way. Sometimes he would just pick one of the guys to push and shove. He had to show that he was no one to challenge. That also covered the fact that I was his property. He wanted everyone to know that, if they came near me, they would pay. He always told me that women were sluts, cunts, pigs and worst of all liars. Sean believed that women could not be trusted; therefore he didn't think that they should be left out of sight.

At one party which all of Sean's gang attended, he had accused me of looking at one of his friends. To Sean this was probably one of the worst violations of his rules in regard to relationships. During that party, he decided to drag me into the main bedroom where, after locking the door, he beat and threatened to kill me until Donny had had enough of my screaming and pleading for help and burst into the room to pull Sean off me where I lay curled in the corner, shaking with fear and relief at the same time.

Years later, Cookie told me that everyone at that party swore that Sean was going to kill me that day. I told her that I, too, shared the same thought although I didn't have any inkling as to what I had done to deserve being treated that way. Actually, I always imagined that it must be my fault. I had very low self-esteem and the continual abuse compounded that image to an all-time low. Each and every time I would break free from Sean, he would either convince me he would change for the better or, if that didn't work, he would terrorize me into accepting him back into my life.

THREE

Relationship Brewing

DURING OUR BREAK-UPS AND MAKE-UPS, the roller coaster separations and reunions, I discovered, at the tender age of sixteen, that I had been impregnated with Sean's child. I suspected something strange was happening within my body when I began to be nauseous all of the time. When my mother would cook dinner, the smell of food would send me into a full-blown retching mode. My breasts were very swollen, tender and sore to the touch. In fact my entire body was taking on a new shape with a hard round ball for a stomach.

I confided in my girlfriends Cookie and Karin. Karin's father was a pharmacist so she was better versed than I when it came to medical issues and Cookie had an array of friends that had already experienced this situation. Basically, there were three choices: abortion, adoption or childbirth. In the end I would ultimately chose the latter of the three even though I was petrified to tell my parents who would, I knew, be disappointed and dismayed. As for telling Sean, our situation had been so volatile, that I knew that this would add fuel to the fire which, in our case, would be more like an inferno.

Sean's reaction was as volatile as his fits of rage. First he questioned the paternity of our child with words that pierced my heart. Needing his assurance and support, as I did, I was crushed. Then, after the few days it took to soak up the news, he came back and after threatening to kill me if the baby wasn't his, began to brag about his upcoming fatherhood to all his older guy friends, like a rooster strutting his stuff after conquering a hen. He bragged to everyone that his sperm was potent. In his mind, this pregnancy validated his manhood. According to Sean he had knocked up his "bitch" or "broad" and that made him a man. This also reaffirmed that I was his property. He decided that, without question, I was carrying and giving birth to his child. His mind was set on his baby. There was only one option then. No abortion for sure and forget adoption too. He told me that, if I killed his baby, he would kill me. Because of that threat I continued to hide my condition from my parents for fear they would force me to some clinic for an abortion. Without so much as a care or a worry on his part about telling our parents, Sean continued to live his life as if everything was normal.

Like a typical teenager, I thought of how this pregnancy might give our love a new light and since I wanted to make our union right and happy, I asked myself why we shouldn't fill it with a baby to love? Then Sean would see how much I cared for him. His anger would turn into tenderness once our baby was born, proof that our love was real.

I was almost six months along before my mother guessed that I was with child and I found that I was greatly relieved that she voiced what I had feared saying all of those months. Afterward, she wiped away her tears and began to discuss my options which, of course, at this stage, did not include abortion as a possibility, thereby making it unnecessary for me to tell her about Sean's threat. Both she and my stepfather were very supportive. My mother told me that she would help me raise the baby, or assist me in adoption procedures, although I made it clear that I wouldn't dream of any other option but to raise my love child. My parent's only stipulations were that I would have to sit down and tell Sean's parents. Aware as she was of Sean's abusive streak, my mother refused to even consider Sean and me getting married, claiming that giving her permission would be equal to signing my death certificate.

We invited Sean's mother, sister and brother over to our house to discuss the arrival of the baby, but not his father, since his parents couldn't stand to be in the same room together. His mother, Dawn, was the more reasonable of the two and they were all very supportive and sympathetic. However, Sean was upset that my family had taken it upon themselves to tell his family of our business. Furthermore, he blamed me for cooperating and said that, by rights, he should cut the baby right out of my belly since, according to his twisted thinking, I somehow didn't deserve to carry his child into this world. This wasn't the last time he would clarify how he felt about me carrying his baby, nor would it be the last bodily threat.

I continued to attend high school and work part time at a fast food restaurant until close to the birth of my child. My mother arranged doctor's appointments, and because she and my stepfather were struggling to make ends meet, medical subsidized assistance was necessary. Still, most of the responsibility for the unborn child fell upon my shoulders. In between all the things on my schedule, I had to find time to handle the fluctuating mood swings from Sean.

During the months of my pregnancy, Sean and I were apart more than we were together, primarily because he acted as if I had somehow trapped him into fatherhood, often lashing out at me so violently that there were times that I hid at my parent's house because I was fearful of him hurting both me and the baby.

During the three months before my due date, Sean's abuse escalated to even more dangerous heights. He continually informed me that I wasn't good enough to give birth to his child and would often go on a rant about how lucky I was that he allowed his child to grow inside of me. Referring to my Italian background, he would call me a half nigger, adding that he couldn't believe that a half nigger was giving birth to his child, and renewed his threats, brandishing a knife, as if to cut the child out of my stomach. And I took his threats seriously. The last time I saw him during my pregnancy was when he pushed me, eight months pregnant, down my parent's basement steps, because I refused to go leave the house with him, causing me to spot blood for three days.

After I told my mother about that incident, she forbade me to see Sean until after the birth of our child. Not that he seemed to mind. As long as he could be sure that I was not running the streets having fun, everything was copasetic in Sean's world. He continued to hang out with his friends and party. Summer was approaching and there was more fun to be had. As for me, I welcomed the break and the security of knowing my baby and I were safe.

On June 20, 1978, I gave birth to a baby girl whom I named Marie Colleen, eighteen inches in length, and weighing six pounds fourteen ounces. She had the thickest black hair I have ever seen, and her skin was dark. Her tiny hands and feet were my first concern. Like every mother,

I had to count the fingers and toes to see that they were all present and accounted for. A strong, healthy, beautiful baby girl, she had a hearty cry and full blast scream. Her little legs kicked non-stop.

There was no doubt that this was Sean's child since she looked just like him. All I keep thinking was that, as soon as he saw her, he would know that I wasn't a cheat or a liar. Over and over, I imagined saying "Here is your little girl, Daddy." Of course, Sean was not present at the hospital for the birth of his daughter, although my mother and stepfather were by my side the entire time. I had phone calls from his family members and visits too. Still there was no Sean. It was a bittersweet experience.

Sean was too busy with his summer fun to be involved with a newborn baby with the result that we didn't set eyes on him for the first months of Marie's life. I was a seventeen year old with a newborn baby girl. I didn't have a job nor did I have any hope of finding one with any future since I only had an eleventh grade education. I was on public assistance from the state of Connecticut. My baby's father, who had decided to ignore the fact that he had a child, was a heroin and alcohol user. All that, coupled with postpartum depression made my future appeared pretty bleak. All my hopes that the baby's birth would bring Sean and me closer together in a storybook ending had come crashing down around me.

Marie was three months old before her father ever held her. Summer was over and Sean had finally succumbed to family pressure to show some responsibility, in the creation of our baby, explaining that the baby didn't really need him, when she was first born. And because I desperately wanted us to become a happy family, I believed him, convinced that I could make it all work.

With this in mind, I decided to move in with Sean at his father's house, despite the fact that his dad had added a roommate to the clan. The roommate was a man with the nickname Parson. He was a priest of some sort and conducted mass at an "Every Faith Church" in Stamford, Connecticut. After living with them for a while, I discovered that Parson favored his wine, a little too excessively. In later years, I heard that Parson died of liver disease which, given his propensity for alcohol, did not come as a surprise.

It was the beginning of a tumultuous existence. In return for caring for him and the baby, Sean showed utter disdain and disgust in regard to any of the choices I made. In Sean's eyes I couldn't do anything the right way. He continually told me that I was a worthless girlfriend and a pathetic mother and it was not long before I began to contemplate ways to escape my nightmare world and would have done so if it had not been for his threats which now included not only myself and my family but the baby.

And so I continued to share a home with three alcoholic men, an incredibly oppressive situation during which Sean broke my spirit. When he was drunk, he would turn into a demonic monster. During these storms of madness, I learned to master the science of timing. For example, when Sean came home from his part time painting job; he would often be annoyed with me for not cooking his dinner properly. It all came to a head, when, deciding to go to the casino with his pals, he discovered that the elastic on his socks was damp. Punching and kicking me, he forced me onto the golf course where I managed to run away, barefooted, to a neighbor's house. The police were called and I had Sean arrested, a huge show of courage on my part. But I had to consider the baby now, and so I fled with her to Sean's sister Colleen's apartment where we lived for a couple of months, and where my daughter celebrated her first birthday at a party which Sean attended after Colleen made him promise to love and respect me. For many years after that Colleen would greet her brother and then say, "You're not hitting that girl are you"?

And so, shortly after Marie's first birthday, I returned to live with Sean. Our reunion began without any major incident, and it was decided that Marie would assume Sean's last name. She was also baptized by Parson at the "Church of Every Faith", located in Stamford, a building situated on a rolling green hill, surrounded by secluded prayer sanctuaries. Off to the side of the property was a small animal farm where an array of small animals had been fenced off to form a petting zoo, for the children. The celebration itself was held, however, at Sean's father's house, and as always when there was a family event, there was excess drinking which led to swearing, cursing and eventually a brawl of some sort. This family function ended with a police report. Sean was arrested early that evening for driving without a license, and being under the influence.

This was the end of the party in many respects. According to Sean, the arrest became everyone else's fault. As usual, blame was placed on other people. Sean dared anyone to disagree. He looked for an argument by being self-righteous. We knew him all too well, to dare argue with his statements, no matter how ridiculous they were. And even though his father had freed him from police custody, Sean attacked him verbally and within minutes the two of them were in a full-fledged physical combat. Things could only be smooth for so long in our world.

It became apparent that my life with Sean was a clip shy of a horror show. Finally realizing that he was incapable of caring for me, I decided that I was done deluding myself regarding my relationship, and that I would no longer mistake fear for love. And yet I could not see how I would escape this dysfunctional trap. I would make a plan and then I would chicken out. The fear of his reprisal crippled my ability to leave him.

Sean's violent temper and outbursts became so frequent that I began to envision the possibility that he might actually kill both me and the baby. It was Cookie that understood my fear the best because Donny behaved the same way toward her. Because of him, her baby had been stillborn. I began sleeping with a knife under my pillow, although the thought of having to use it terrified me.

The day that turned my life upside-down was when my mother and I went shopping and I bought a red dress for our baby. I didn't even think about the color when I made the purchase. Marie had dark hair so the color red complimented her complexion. Not so in Sean's opinion.

When I arrived home that evening, he immediately began berating me about the color, threatening to kill me if I ever dressed the baby in red again. According to him, red was only worn by whores. It was then that he attacked, threatening to kill the both of us, as he ripped the red dress off the child, using the sharp tip of the knife. It was at that pivotal moment that I know this was all I needed to gather enough courage to leave. It was on that day that I know in my heart that I would not survive if I remained in that house. The fact that Sean would endanger our baby's well-being shocked me into true reality. It took Sean threatening my daughter, for me to take serious action on our behalf.

That evening I slept with one eye open, and one hand curled around the handle of a knife hidden under my pillow and prayed for god's protection. During the night, each time Sean stirred, my heart throbbed. It took this entire night to map out my plan of escape. I kept in mind the numerous threats he had made on my family in the event of my leaving him but I know that they as adults were capable of self-preservation. My first priority was protecting the baby. My focus was on how I could permanently remove us from harm's way.

Finally, I decided that I had no other choice but to run away as far as I could go. I made this decision knowing, that Sean would be enraged at my escape as he always had been when I had tried before. On many occasions his game of cat and mouse had deterred me from running, knowing as I did that, when he caught me, my punishment would be even worse than it would have been had I stayed. The fact that I ran away would fester in him, like a boil just waiting to erupt, and now I knew that the poison that spilled out of that boil would surely be fatal to me if he could find me. Therefore, I had to make this my last time, to run away to long-term safety.

FOUR

Escape Violence

DAWN ARRIVED IN SLOW MOTION, or so it seemed, and my heart raced with the anticipation of the new day's plan for our flight to freedom and design of survival. When Sean stirred, I pretended that I was asleep for fear of rehashing the scene from the previous night, remaining motionless, as I waited for him to leave the house.

The moment Sean stepped off the front step; I quickly collected our belongings and ran to my daughter who was sleeping so peacefully, untainted by the fear that rose in my throat. As I dressed her and gathered our things, I promised myself that I would always keep her safe and that we would leave that house never to return. As I drove away, half an hour later, I pressed my foot a bit heavier on the gas petal and the adrenaline soared through my body as I realized how much horror and sadness I had experienced there, knowing that there was no other option but to go forward. I wanted to get as far away from him as I possibly could. The farther away I drove the more I imagined that he would somehow know my plan, and be following behind me, conditioned as I was to thinking he was in my head and knew my thoughts and plans for escape. I had to keep reminding myself that he did not know my plan, nor would he have any idea where I had gone.

I drove to my friend Cookie's house and begged her to watch Marie for me while I went shopping, telling her that my mother would pick Marie up later that day. I kissed my baby goodbye and whispered that I loved her and I would see her real soon. As those words left my lips, my heart sank as I realized that I might not fulfill that promise. It would be Sean that caused my demise, the fate of circumstances.

I was off to my mother's house to gather a few things and write her a note in which I explained that I was leaving Sean and asked her to pick Marie up as soon as she got off work, adding that I had a plan for a peaceful safe new beginning, and stressing the importance of keeping all of it top secret. And since my mother was all too familiar with abuse and the escalation of danger, I had confidence in her ability to protect my daughter and care for her, until I was in a safe place.

Sean was unfamiliar with my paternal father and his residence, my father and I having been estranged, ever since I went to live with my mother and stepfather. My oldest sister Joan lived in small bungalow up the street from my father's house in Greenwich and this was, I thought, a perfect hideaway for me until I could decide on a more permanent relocation.

When I arrived at my sister's house, she tried to reassure me that I was safe with her, and when I called my mother at work, she assured me that no harm would come to her grandchild, and that she would go and get Marie immediately. Then I had to call Cookie to make sure that Marie was safe and to tell her that my mother would pick her up soon. Obviously aware that something was as wrong, Cookie begged me to tell her where I was and to explain what Sean had done to me this time, being all too familiar of the treatment I was in store for if he caught up with me. I told her about the entire incident, but I refused to disclose my location on the grounds that what she didn't know, Sean could not force out of her.

I knew in my heart that I had to begin all over again. I had to design a whole new life. I had to live in a different place and I could not mix the old and the new. Even my former friends could not be privy to my identity in this new life. I had to wash away the old Margo and begin anew.

Although my daughter was safely secured at my mother's house, I still worried that Sean would strike out against them to get to me. He had attacked his own parents and siblings, so it seemed reasonable to assume that no one was exempt from his fury. I kept calling my parents to reassure myself that Sean did not know where Marie was. My mother was very concerned that I rest and reach a calmer state before she brought my daughter to me.

Later that evening I called Cookie who told me that when Sean came home and found out that I was gone, he'd gone ballistic, becoming even more violent but that she was able to convinced him that she did not know where I was. Feeling doomed, I cried for hours for myself and for my baby, I was a prisoner of my own imagination. And although I was exhausted, I couldn't sleep.

When Joan went out to the store to pick up a few groceries, I searched the bathroom cabinet for pain relievers for my headache and instead I found a bottle of nerve pills. At that time, I decided that it would be easier on everyone involved if I took the whole bottle. Convinced that I would finally be free from Sean by removing myself from the equation, I swallowed the entire bottle of pills and awoke in the emergency ward of the local hospital with tubes up my nose and a wrenching pain in my abdomen. My mother was by my side, holding my hand, and my sister was sitting on the foot of the bed sobbing, "Thank god you woke up. It's all my fault. I should have never left you alone". The social worker had been in and spoken with my mother regarding the situation, and I was finally released in the care of my mother.

Later that day, I returned to my mother's house to reunite with my daughter and to gather all of our belongings. From there I would go to live with my sister to begin a new life. I held my baby and was filled with joy. For a brief moment I didn't have any other care but to hold this innocent child. She gave me the strength to trudge forward. She was the force behind my flight to survive, and I knew that she would always give me the determination, strength and courage to fight.

With my mother listening on the other line, I took a deep breath and dialed Sean's phone number, prepared to tell him that I was severing our relationship. It was no surprise to me that he reverted to his usual response, beginning with pleas for forgiveness, and going on to claim that he could not live without us, to threats of suicide, to threats leveled at me and my family and when I did not respond, reverted to repeating, "Margo, now I know that you love me, please don't leave me," which led me to gain enough courage to tell him that I had only fear in my heart for him, and that the love I had once felt had been beaten out of me. I went on to say that I was going to my uncle's home in Michigan at which he screamed,"

I'm coming for you, bitch! You can run but you can't hide forever," before slamming the phone down.

My mother immediately called the police while I gathered up my belongings, sobbing hysterically. The officers arrived and were escorting me from the house when Sean came driving up. While they restrained him, I heard him shout, "I don't care how long it takes me, I will find you and when I do, I'll kill you. So you better look behind you, every single day, because one day, when you least expect it, I'll be there"! Those words haunted me for many years.

Convinced that Sean thought I was on my way to Michigan, I continued to live with Joan. And although I was free of Sean physically, the psychological scars he had inflicted would haunt me for a long time. I remained Sean's captive in a web of psychological warfare in which I had to remain hidden in the new world. I had created for myself, during which I took every precaution imaginable to ensure our safety. I ceased all of the state's financial assistance because that was a direct link to my new living arrangements and lived in seclusion, detaching myself from all of my past connections with people and places. As far as anyone was aware, I had moved to Michigan to start a new life.

Determined to be a responsible provider, I joined my sister in obtaining our GED. My stepmother watched my daughter, as I worked in the evenings as a salesgirl for a local department store. When I discovered a grant program being implemented by the federal government, I applied for trade school and was accepted with the result that I attended beauty school full time during the day, and kept my job at night. On my off hours, I remained focused and close to home, and tried to forget Sean, something that was made more difficult because of the threatening calls that he made to my parents, news of which spun me backward into that world of fear and worry. Gradually, however, I learned to tuck these emotions far down in my mind, so far that I could almost convince myself that they didn't exist. It was my way of surviving.

After a while my parents felt the situation would improve if they thought about moving. Placing their house on the market, they sold it and moved to another address and acquired an unlisted telephone number to avoid further harassment from Sean. I remember feeling so relieved that my family would finally be safe from him.

As time progress, when there were no more phone calls to report or threatening statements to disclose, I prayed it was over. As the months passed, I focused on rebuilding my life which meant concentrating on cultivating positive self-confidence and self-esteem. I became extremely goal oriented for now failure was not an option.

FIVE

New Identity

ALL THESE PAST EXPERIENCES PAVED the way for yet another chapter in my life. I had found the courage to traverse a new world, in the process of which, I had adopted a brand new identity. I took the road ahead, with all of its twists and turns, in my stride. I had the ingredient for a good life at my fingertips. The first phase had already begun and I moved into the second with a gleeful heart.

During the time that I attended beauty school, I met a handsome young Jewish man with sea-green eyes and jet black curls. Tall and slim, he dressed with a designer touch from his jewelry to his shoes. I didn't realize it then, but this man would turn out to be the key to my new identity, setting me free from my old world of fear and worry.

Scott Saunders was his name, and what with his kindness and sincerity, he was a far cry from the kind of tough guy I had attracted before. Right from the start, he showed a great deal of interest in me as a person, making it clear that he found me attractive and funny. Even more important, he accepted the fact that I had a two-year-old child and seemed excited to meet her. As we continued to date and I shared some of my past experiences with him, he showed extreme empathy and support.

Six months later, Scott and I announced our intent to marry to our parents. Mine were delighted to welcome such a nice man into our family, but his parents were hesitant because we were not only young, but not yet financially stable, a special consideration because of Marie. However, once they realized that we were determined to wed, they adjusted to the idea.

As for me, I was ecstatic, not only because I loved Scott, but also because this marriage was my opportunity to free my daughter and myself from Sean's identifying and tracking us down. Scott, now my key to safety and protection from Sean, promised to adopt Marie, and vowed to love her as he would love his own child. We seemed to be on the brink of the sort of life I had always wanted.

Scott, who came from an upper middle class Jewish family, had grown up in the affluent suburbs of Connecticut, a bit privileged and spoiled by his mother. His father was a very successful businessman who held a high managerial position for a major department store's corporation and was a levelheaded and practical parent who did not over indulge his children. Both of Scott's parents, extremely involved as they were in the affairs of the local temple, were dedicated to their Jewish heritage. His father was even on the board of the local reform synagogue.

Scott's older brother, Saul, had graduated from the City's University and was living in the Bronx at the time, and although he originally agreed with his parents that we ought not to jump into marriage too quickly, I soon won his affection and approval.

Scott and I were both licensed beauticians, who eventually worked together in a high end salon in Darien, Connecticut. Our positions were assistants to a master hairstylist there, referred to her by her sister who was a teacher in the beauty college. After I had acquired the position, I listened for any upcoming assistant positions that came available and when one of the salon owners wanted to replace his current assistant, Scott applied and was accepted. He had great charismatic charm coupled with his newly developing talent. It was more than enough to land this job and future career possibilities.

Our new life was good. Because our financial resources were limited, we decided to live with Scott's parents until we saved enough money to have a decent beginning. After six months, we moved into a modest apartment complex near to that area. It would top the long list of addresses we would acquire to avert the possibility of Sean finding us.

I was so grateful to Scott for providing Marie and me with a stable environment that I tended to ignore any potential marital problems, some of which sprang from financial hardship which spurred us on to put in as many as twelve hours a day at the salon. I was determined to be successful, in our marriage and career.

After five years of hard work and dedicated training, I reached my full potential. My clientele quadrupled in numbers and we were able to comfortably support our daughter in a fashion that I had formerly only dreamt of. Scott was a young man who sacrificed his youth by becoming a responsible father of a three-year-old toddler.

Over the years of struggling, Scott and I had many conversations regarding my past situation in order to be constantly alert to the danger, which Sean posed, and were always very careful. We moved often enough, always without leaving a forwarding address to make it impossible for him to trace us. When Scott adopted Marie, my attorney informed us that the adoption would require Sean's signature and approval. The legal document would also list our new name. But since, after I went through with the adoption, we moved again, I felt safe.

I also became quite adept at keeping my past a secret. While at work, I told my clientele that I was five years older than my actual age to throw people off, and never answered questions about where I had grown up, changing the subject as quickly as I could. And if, on rare occasions, I encountered someone from my past, I went out of my way to avoid him or her. Once when coming face-to-face with a former schoolmate, I had no alternative but to request that she not repeat to anyone who knew Sean that she had seen me. Another time, I was on the Seaside Heights' boardwalk, standing in one of the clothing stores, when I saw Sean himself walking down the boardwalk, whereupon I completely panicked and ran with my daughter and hid under a circular clothing rack in the store. My daughter thought it was a game, but I knew it was a matter of life or death and remained under the rack, terrified, until I felt the coast was clear. After that, having been reminded that I was not completely safe from Sean, I was much more cautious of where I went and of who was in my immediate path. Diving deeper into my new identity, I pushed the frightening memories of my former life into the back corners of my mind. I honestly wanted to erase those memories completely.

Meanwhile, I latched on to all of the traditions that made Scott's family what they were. Scott's family lovingly accepted Marie and I into their hearts and as authentic family members. Feeling that I needed to become a legitimate member of the Jewish faith, I studied all of the customs and laws of the religion and was converted into the Jewish religion. I attended services each and every Shabbat, and observed all our holidays, even enrolling Marie in Sunday school at the temple.

In doing all this, I was developing a strong sense of worth and identity. The fact that now I belonged to something greater than myself enabled me to tuck my real background farther away in my mind. As far as I was concerned, the firmer the grip on my present the farther away my past would travel. Isolation from my past, including, sadly, my family, was my way of making my new life more real.

We had escaped Sean and his violent way of life, but my new life had its own bitter lessons as well. Having met my goals and become successful in my profession, I was appalled when my marriage plunged into a sudden nosedive. One reason, perhaps, was that I had gradually paid less and less attention to my personal life. Over the years, Scott and I became resentful of one another. The very attributes that we each admired in the other at the beginning of our union were the very things that we despised about each other later on. My unwavering drive and determination to succeed which, Scott had once admired later turned into resentment. His gentleness that I had once found so appealing later created bitterness toward him. I ignored the falling pieces of my once beautiful beginning and allowed my tunnel vision of career success to damage my relationship.

In fact, I felt that Scott pushed me to work harder because he knew it was the fuel that sparked my existence. He wanted to help me figure out how to multiple my clientele. Scott's intentions were to cultivate my drive and talent and I mistook his assistance as pressure to perform. As a young couple with a ready-made family we had many responsibilities that added to the dissolution of our union. It was certainly true enough that our fast pace lifestyle, immaturity and struggle to succeed eroded our little family. Since we were both stubborn, disputes happened between us spreading the gap between the three of us. A battle of wills became the norm in our home. Often times Scott and I were at odds with picking the same path for the raising of our child. I tried not to pick sides. At the time, I was unable to understand why they were always in competition for the number one spot in my world. In retrospect, the real reason was that my time and attention was on my career first and my family second. It was my learned way of survival.

Scott, being a young man trying to find his niche in the work world, had changed careers several times. He was extremely talented in sales and with managing people and had a great deal of knowledge about the business world, but I didn't always support him emotionally, in discovering his place in the business world. Meanwhile, his parents, realizing how financially rewarding our endeavor was, decided to invest in the beauty business, to guarantee our family a stable future. For a while it seemed like the perfect arrangement.

But, as our business grew more prosperous, our marriage began to fail, our daily communication limited as it was to business issues only; Scott and I constantly disagreed. In the end, we worked together all day long and then argued bitterly about the business to which I dedicated all my attention behind a hairstylist' chair, and he dedicated his attention to the business aspect of our growing salon.

Our communication was equal to that of strangers passing by one another. We had a fast paced life filled with fancy cars, jewels, furs, expensive vacations and parties. Our lifestyle was beyond what our maturity level could handle. It seems that the more material things we obtained, the further we drifted apart. Unfortunately, in so doing; I lost my life, as I had known it to be.

Within two years to the day of the salon's anniversary, our marriage had completely dissolved. We had lived on a forty-acre farm with all the trimmings, including horses, bunnies, chickens and a family dog name Bernard, the perfect picture of the setting for a happy marriage. But with our union's dissolution, I lost it all. I had just turned twenty-five, and had once again to figure out how to start my life over. After finding a new place for my daughter and me to live, I found work at a salon named Main Line Salon located down the street from the one Scott and I had operated, now owned, by one of our former employees, while Scott and his' mistress quickly moved to Florida.

One of my major disappointments in regard to that break up was the realization that I had lost my second identity, having failed at my attempt to live a normal life. In my mind I was a public joke, a true flunky. All that I had worked for had been stripped away. I had crashed miserably at my attempt for a new life. And even though I refused to give up Scott's name, our break-up made me vulnerable again. My career was my only hope for survival. I refused to acknowledge the emptiness inside myself, although I realized that I had lost an established relationship, one that was once based on mutual respect and genuine love. I had spent years working on my outward appearance and measured my worthiness on my financial status, trying to fill the emptiness inside me with material wealth. But it had all been a delusion instead of a true reflection of what was really important.

In those days the money was plentiful, however. My exterior world was filled with diamonds and furs, fancy cars, beach houses and winter ski houses. I ran wild and free to do as I wished. I hired babysitters and lived what I expected to be the "Good Life". My girlfriends and I frequented many late nightclubs during those disco days. We danced until dawn. I took exotic vacations to different parts of the world. I dated guys none of which were serious relationships, since not many men wanted to be involved with a woman in her twenties who was also a mother of a nine-year-old child. Perhaps because of that, I never encountered a man who was interested in a long-term exclusive partnership. I was in my late twenties and the same applied to the men I dated who, because of my daughter, I never quite meshed with. Instead I connected to older people, because their life experience allowed me to have more in common with their interests. Therefore, I had on and off relationships, filled with men who were needy and required extensive care taking.

Gradually, my daughter and I grew apart, each of us living in our own separate worlds of promise and survival. She remained in contact with her father Scott, and because I wanted her have a close relationship with him, I allowed her to fly to and from Florida. I hadn't had any success in establishing a complete loving relationship. My emotional well-being was at an all-time low. My life was consumed by loneliness; my career was the only successful aspect in my world. Marie insisted on the idea that her father and I belonged together. I began to consider the possibility of Scott and I becoming a family again. The thought of a reunion had added appeal because my mother, who was only fifty, had been operated on for heart disease, which added to my depression and reexamination of how my life had plummeted. And so I accepted Scott's invitation and sought out the comfort and stability of Scott's world.

We rarely spoke of our past problems or the causes of our breakup, no doubt because Scott and I both had hit rock bottom while estranged from one another, both submerging ourselves in other people's lives. We had experimented with alcohol and drugs of all different kinds but nothing could fulfill the void in our lives. Now we thought that our reunion would do the trick. Although I believed that Scott's intentions were honest and honorable, I didn't fully believe in the strength of our remarriage, and I was right. Two years after reigniting our marriage vows, we agreed on an amicable divorce.

My daughter was now a teenager, her hormones raging, her attitude at its all-time worst. The confusion of Scott and I uniting, reuniting and separating again had left her very angry and rebellious. The relationship between her father and herself became increasingly dark while hers and mine became an ongoing battle of wills. We tried therapy and a new approach to those angry feelings inside her, while at the same time, I attempted to maintain my career and master the difficult task of being a single parent, making the mistake of replacing all that I thought was missing in her life with pretty things. This was how I learned to show my affection and achieve acceptance. As her relationship with her father faltered, I watched my daughter's pain. I felt that I had failed her as a mother and tried to fill the gap with freedom of choice and leniency, intent on becoming her friend rather than her mother, all the time trying to ignore the emptiness I felt inside.

Marie moved along the path of her own discovery, while I struggled down my own. We both developed a great need for acceptance and love from outside sources, which created problems for the both of us individually, and as a family unit, meanwhile attracting, on my part, a series of weak, needy men which, far from strengthening my relationship with my daughter, created even more distance between us. Soon our relationship was filled with blame, bitterness, jealousy and competition, all of which created a thick wall between us. Marie interpreted my personal relationships as an invasion of her world, and an intrusion upon her needs and desires. Her demands became so great that it sometime seemed that my personal life had to be put on hold altogether.

Marie tried to drive a wedge between me and any man in my life by being ill mannered and disrespectful. The closer I came to a man, the harder Marie would work to separate us. I remember breaking up with one of my boyfriends after being honest with him regarding Marie, explaining that she wanted my exclusive attention, at least until she went off to college, and that I had come to the conclusion my life would be more peaceful, if I just went with the flow.

My monogamous existence seemed to make my daughter happy. And since she was very social, I attended to her every need and desire, my only outlet being my work and the gym. From the outside, it I seemed like I had the world on a chain. People viewed me as well put together and happy with a bubbly personality. No one could see my loneliness, my insecurities, and my desperation to be loved. I would not allow anyone to see my weakness, to know that I was vulnerable. I put on a happy face and a smile to disguise the painful wounds inside my mind and heart. Always a happy face . . .

SIX

Nightmare Relived

My nightmare became reality on an ordinary October day, in 1992. At this juncture in the road I worked at a salon in Darien, Connecticut called La Mes Salon. The receptionist had just introduced me to a new client whom I had begun to consult about a new hair design when I was interrupted by an incoming call which I assumed was from my teenage daughter or my housekeeper since theirs were the extent of phone calls I received at work. I always answered, because my daughter's chronic asthma condition.

To my surprise, this particular call was from my mother whose voice was shaking. This was not typical for my mother was so strong that all of my siblings swore she was made of stone. Now her words swirled around in my head like a swarm of bees. Each word she uttered stung feverously, even though she was clearly trying to remain calm as she told me that Sean had returned to make good on his promises made fourteen years earlier. It seemed that Sean had gone to my Uncle Johnny' house with another guy, and held a meat cleaver to my uncle and his five year son's necks while demanding to speak with me. My Uncle Johnny had called her and she had told Sean that if he left her brother alone, she would make sure that I contacted him, refusing, however, to give him my phone number or address. "Tell that bitch that I'm back!" he had told her as he slammed down the receiver.

All my memories suddenly became vibrantly real, and I ran to my boss's back office, electrified with nervous energy and tried to explain to him all of what was happening, attempting to make sense of a senseless situation. I cried and spoke quickly in an attempt to relay the impeding danger I was in. I asked him to have someone take my clientele for the rest of the day and then cancel my bookings for the next couple of weeks, not bothering to listen to his response, eager to call my housekeeper and warn her of the possible danger. I had to get her and my daughter out of that house, in the event Sean found out where I really lived.

I left work that day with the intention of running as far away as I could in order to protect my loved ones. I had to ensure my daughter's safety. My mind sped through many different memories of my past with Sean. Suddenly I was stuck in a state of shock with the reality of it all. My thoughts then raced to the possibility of Sean knowing everything about me. I even went as far as to imagine that Sean had knowledge of my route home. These were some of the crazy thoughts that passed through my mind while driving down the back roads to my Darien home. Was it possible that he could read my mind? Did he know my next move? Had he follow me from work to watch how I would run scared? I kept looking frantically in my rear-view mirror expecting every time to find him behind me, instantly reverting to become the paranoid person I had once been.

Different scenes flashed before my eyes, some of which I had experienced, and some I imagined I was yet to suffer. How would I relay the details of this volatile situation to my daughter, my housekeeper and lastly the local police department? This was a tough predicament. The only thing I was certain of was that I must run as far away as possible and quickly. Once I was safe, I would then be able to figure out another method of protection.

I arrived home with only half of my sanity intact, and after giving my daughter and housekeeper some idea of what had happened, called the Darien police department and reported Sean's threats. Then I had to gather up my belongings and my daughter's things and go to the station to file an official report, as well as to request a gun permit. I also made a few calls to different alarm companies, and scheduled an appointment for the installation of a high tech home alarm. And since I had no intention of living at that house unprotected until the alarm was installed, and I was equipped with all the bells and whistles, I called a local locksmith and ordered a dead bolt lock to be installed on my bedroom door for extra protection and called an electrician to install motion detection lights outside my property.

Determined to be thorough, I had a gardener to cut down all bushes and tree branches that obstructed my view, or could have served as a hiding spot for Sean and made a phone call to my daughter's school to inform them of her absence in the coming weeks. I left them with strict instructions that, when she returned, no one was authorized to take my daughter from school, with the exception of mother, my housekeeper or myself, briefly explaining the reason why it was so important that they adhere to my request. This was a safety issue for all of us involved.

Then I called a former boyfriend, Bobby Schwinn, who worked at local international airline, explained the situation and had him check if he could get me plane tickets out of New York to Florida as soon as possible. After he was able to arrange a flight for two days later, I called two close friends, Carry and Clark, who lived in Florida and was relieved when Carry was gracious enough to extend their home to us, for as long as it was necessary.

After I had everything set for a safe shelter, the last thing I had to do was call my mother to hear how it was that Sean had found my uncle and exactly what he knew about me, or whether or not she thought that Sean was coming to my house as well as how much time I had remaining before I fled, and was told that Sean had met a girl named Laura, a friend of Joan's at a party in one of the Bronx neighborhoods, where he resided. And although she no longer kept in touch with my older sister, she was friendly with my estranged Uncle Johnny, my mother's brother, one of whose friends she had dated, a girl who hadn't seen any harm in telling Sean where my uncle lived.

It was a few days later, when Sean and another guy, showed up at my uncle Johnny's front door, and grabbing him in a choke-hold, demanded that he get his cunt niece on the phone. My uncle was so rattled by this unexpected attack that he could not remember the number and had to call my aunt who alerted the Bronx police department of the hostage situation. Meanwhile, my other uncle, Teddy, who was in from Michigan visiting my aunt, ran over to my Uncle Johnny's house to help him, arriving at the same time as the police who, as they told me later, Sean confronted, as brazen as ever, with a barely concealed knife in his pocket.

"There's no problem here officers, right, John?" he said. "Tell them there's no problem."

My uncle was all too familiar with how the city streets demand a certain behavior, and that being a rat to the police was a sure way of being killed. As far as he knew, Sean had connections with a gang who could, even if he was arrested, come back and harm his family. And so he acted accordingly, with the result that the police left after giving Sean a warning.

Years later, my Uncle Teddy was still telling about how menacing Sean had been. Although he had served as a career officer in the armed services and had come across many dangerous situations he never forgot how Sean had behaved that night. As for my Uncle John, years later, he was still haunted by what he viewed as his inability to "off Sean" for good.

By the time my mother finished telling me everything that had happened, I was totally drained of every emotion except fear. Finishing my packing, I locked up the house, gave the housekeeper a big hug and thanked her for helping me, after which Marie and I drove away from our house and from the life we had known forever. Tears streamed down my cheeks, as I raced off to the police station, to file my report.

Seven

Seek Protection

I DROVE THROUGH THE STREETS of Darien, as if I were on a high-speed chase, unable to get to the police station fast enough. Marie had only known my former husband, Scott, as her father. Six months prior to all of this current turmoil, she had just discovered, during an angry exchange with him over the phone, that he was her adopted father. Scott had later explained that he had said it out of frustration and anger, but regardless of what prompted his reaction, Marie would carry this heart-breaking pain in her heart. And now it is difficult to imagine the horror with which she had discovered that her biological father was a danger to both of us.

Still shaken, I arrived at the police station and was introduced to a Detective Wyatt who listened with obvious disbelief, as I hysterically recounted my story, interrupting occasionally to verify a fact and telling me so often to calm down and that the police would handle everything that I suspected that he did not understand how urgent the threat from Sean was. Gradually, however, he seemed to become a little more concerned with the seriousness of the circumstance, especially when I told him about how I had fled from Sean fourteen years earlier with the help of the Stamford Police Department. When I told him about how I had established a new identity, I was compelled to share the full impact of how Sean's behavior toward my family, including my Uncle Johnny, had constituted a sincere intent to cause harm. In an attempt to make him aware that Sean's violent demands did not equal an idle threat, I kept saying that Sean had promised, on the day I left him, that he would find me, and then he would get me no matter how long it took. I wanted the police to know that no one hunts down someone after fourteen years, unless they are serious about hurting them.

In the end, Detective Wyatt did place my house on red tag alert, which meant that, if a call came in from my address, an extra warning alert would be implemented which would cause the police to take more immediate precautions than they might have done earlier. Furthermore, once I installed my alarm system, it would be directly linked to the police department by the alarm company. I informed the detective of my planned absence from my house until the alarm was fully activated and discussed my intentions for the installation extra locks deadbolts, shrub removal and outside motion lights and the appointments for each protective measure.

Detective Wyatt did advise me not to file a restraining order because, on that order, it would be necessary to list my current address. I then inquired about filing for a permit for the purchase of a firearm, but Detective Wyatt told me that I didn't need a gun, insisting that the police department would be satisfactory protection. I knew then that I hadn't gotten through to him in regard to how dangerous Sean was as far as Marie and I were concerned and reiterated my need and desire to protect myself immediately if Sean reappeared. "You don't realize what you're dealing with," I told him. "Sean will kill me before you get into your cars before leaving the police department." But he was obdurate. In the end, I asked the women at the window for an application for a permit to purchase a firearm which would, she informed me, take four to six months from the date of application to obtain. I filled out the application and submitted it to her, in spite of the lengthy time limitations and the opposition of Detective Wyatt and left the station feeling not only misunderstood, but frightened and alone, my only option being to run away again since it would be two days before Marie and I could be on a plane to Florida. And although I had never wanted to have this conversation with my daughter, I explained what had happened during my life with her father, and saw, to my disappointment, that she saw him as a rather glamorous, exciting figure, all of which should have constituted a warning to me if my focus had not been on our immediate flight to safety.

Our first refuge was at the house of my good friends Megan and Anthony who set up their basement for our arrival. It was comfortable and private enough for Marie and me to feel at home. The fact that they had an alarm system in their place was comforting, and Anthony assured me that we were completely safe there. He also arranged for me to meet with a friend of his, a retired detective with whom I could discuss several safety options on the one night we would be staying with them.

I spoke with my mother several times throughout the day and told her what was transpiring in respect to a plan of escape, as well as letting her know all of the details from the police report to the appointments set up at my house for increased security. I told her that I was going to call Sean as he had requested, so that he would stop terrorizing my uncle. However, I couldn't call him until I worked up enough courage and I wasn't there yet; I thought that maybe the following day I would be calm enough to attempt that feat.

That evening, Anthony's friend, the detective, arrived and after hearing my story, advised me to obtain a gun for protection and, speaking as a friend, explained that there were ways of getting around the need for a gun permit all of which validated my suspicions that I was not going to get much protection from the authorities which was all the more reason for Marie and I getting out of town quickly before Sean found us.

The next day I made plans to stay at a hotel for that evening on the grounds that I would be safer there. But first I had to protect my uncle by calling Sean as I had promised. I had his phone number on a piece of paper. It was the number my mother had recited to me over the phone the previous day when he had made his raid on my uncle's house. I stared at that paper on and off all day long while trying to work up enough nerve to dial that number.

Megan, Anthony and Marie were all present when I dialed the Sean's number. In my mind, I had been rehearsing what I would say to him for the entire day. When the phone rang, I took a deep breath and fixed my mind on sounding tough, reminding myself that it was only a phone call and that he could not jump through the line and get us. Over and over again the phone rang and my heartbeat tripled its normal rhythm.

When Sean finally answered, he seemed disorientated, as though he were drunk or drugged. At first he failed to comprehend who I was, confusing me with my mother and threatening to kill her brother if she didn't tell him where his daughter was. When I told him I was Margo, he seemed to fall apart.

"You cunt," he shouted. "I told you I'd be back. Where the fuck is my daughter? Where the fuck is she, bitch? You don't think I know about that Jew bastard you married, twice. He must have had a big cock. Don't think I've forgotten that you gave my daughter a Jew's name. She is no fuckin Jew! Tell that Jew bastard I'm coming for him, too, you cunt!"

I recoiled from the receiver as if it had bitten me, and then, trying to remain focused and calm, I was determined to keep my voice from quivering, I told Sean that I wasn't afraid of him and that, unless he left my uncle alone, he would never speak to his daughter again. On the other hand, if he promised to leave Uncle Johnny alone, I would let her talk to him now.

When Sean realized it was Marie on the phone, he immediately changed his tone to one of affection, in a conversation which ended with her promising to stay in touch with him if he promised to stop threatening her family. This was her first encounter with her biological father, but, unfortunately, it would not be her last. Shaken, we left for the hotel where Bobby, my present significant other, met me with our plane tickets. Marie really liked him better than anyone I had dated over the years. She felt a connection to him, a friendship of sorts, and his being present at the hotel gave us both comfort and a feeling of security. He was extremely upset for both of us and wanted to help any way he could, with the exception of getting pummeled by Sean. That secure feeling only lasted a few hours, and then Bobby left us to go home. We were alone again to count down the hours until take off.

The next morning we checked out of the hotel and checked into another before leaving for the airport. All my safety plans were put into motion for home security improvements prior to us taking off. I had doubled checked all of the appointments, especially the alarm company. I spoke with my mother to find out the status of my uncle, relieved to find that Sean had not turned up at his house again. I only hoped that it would continue to remain peaceful on the home front.

Marie and I drove to the New York Airport and boarded a plane destined for Florida. As the wheels of our plane left the ground, a blanket of calm enveloped me, and by the time our plane landed in Florida, I was already much more at ease than I had been for days. My friends Clark and Carry picked us up at the airport and drove us to their house in Boca Raton, and under the rays of the hot sun, my fears completely melted.

Two weeks away really cured my yearning to be secure, so much so, in fact, that it was easier for me to return to Connecticut where, to my relief, I found that all of the security precautions had been implemented with the result that my house was as close to a fortress as it could get. I parked my Jimmy 4x4 in the driveway after backing into the spot, so that my driver's door would be lined up with the entrance door to my house, forming one straight path to safety.

I had to return to work and my nerves were on edge, although while I had been gone, Sean had not harassed my family. That was one of the factors that allowed me to continue my life. I thought that it was a good possibility that he had simply been curious, and had been satisfied with the phone call from Marie. I wanted desperately to believe that, as fast and furious as Sean appeared, he would disappear just as suddenly. I kept in close contact with my mother with updates on the situation, and made sure that all of the authorities were abreast of the situation, including my local police station and Marie's school.

Often, I would run into a local police officer named Percy Packs who had come to my house on several occasions when my daughter suffered asthma attacks and required emergency attention. Once he knew about my security precautions, Officer Packs told me to make sure those motion lights were on because he didn't want to get killed by Sean while responding to an emergency call. One day, when my girlfriend Lori and I were lunching at a local diner, Officer Packs appeared and came over to ask about Sean, and when I said that he had threatened my uncle in the Bronx, he said something I would never forget." Shoot him and then make sure you drag him in the house," he told me. "We'll take care of the rest." I was taken aback from his statement, particularly since it reinforced my opinion of the lack of support offered by our legal system. And when, via my mother, I discovered that Sean was still threatening my Uncle Johnny, I decided that I had to equip myself with a gun, which, after having been rebuffed by the police department once again, I managed through the good offices of my friend, Denise's husband Phil who had signed me up for an Aikido self-defense courses the previous year, and who now loaned me a handgun together with a box of bullets.

When my grandmother passed away, I had to go into the South Bronx to her funeral. Of course, her death notice was posted in the local newspaper's obituary column. Although, my grandmother had a different last name, I was still afraid that Sean would show up at her funeral and so I carried the gun with me into the funeral parlor and into the Catholic Church as well, after saying a prayer to God, asking for his understanding. I mention this to demonstrate that I carried that gun everywhere. When seven months passed without Sean continuing to accost my uncle, I felt secure enough to return the gun to Phil, because it had served its purpose. At last I felt that I was living in a normal environment. But as it turned out, this was a temporary false sense of comfort which all suddenly changed in late June of 1993.

Sean's return to my uncle's deli together with his friend T-Hawk turned the tables upside down. They demanded that my uncle give me two phone numbers and to instruct me to have my daughter call him, breaking some chairs to show they meant business, before they left. As it turned out, Sean's father had had a stroke, and they no longer lived together. Sean had changed his phone number and in the event that he had to move again, he gave his mother's phone number as an extra contact. I was astounded when I found out that he had vandalized my uncle's workplace and even more astonished, when I called his mother's phone number and she informed me that my daughter had been calling Sean, for the past seven months. That, of course, explained why there had been no harassment recently.

Unbeknownst to me, Marie had copied Sean's phone for her own private use. A curious teenager, she had many issues with her adopted father Scott's absence, including rebellion. Certainly, she didn't understand the serious dangers that she had so freely invited into our lives by contacting Sean. Rationality seemed to have no influence on her decision making when it came to him, no doubt because she wanted so badly to have a father in her life, to be loved by her real dad. Since Sean had so thunderously returned to avenge the people who had taken his daughter away from him, his image appeared to be one of a heroic noble knight in Marie's mind.

When I talked to her about this, I discovered that she wasn't really concerned with the fact that her actions had put us in harm's way. Her focus was her desire to know who Sean really was, in the process of which she actually downplayed the fact that he was a threat to our safety. During the months of speaking with her, he had convinced Marie that the whole world was against him and his character was almost lamb like. I knew Sean well enough to know how convincing he could be, especially to an adolescent. He had actually made her believe, despite all the evidence to the contrary, that he was harmless.

However, Marie's curiosity was, as I learned later, short-lived, and when over a month passed without her calling him, Sean, paranoid as usual and convinced that I had prevented her from contacting him even though, in reality, I had no idea at the time that they had been in touch, began to torment my uncle again.

Although I felt betrayed by her eagerness to call him and was frightened about what she had let slip about our whereabouts, I sat Marie down and tried not to be too harsh with her while, at the same time, trying to explain the danger of establishing contact with her father. In retrospect, I understand her actions and inquisitive behavior, along with her desperate need to feel loved by her paternal father, but at that time, I was outraged and upset with her lack of concern for our well being. In the end, I made her promise that she would never call Sean again without my permission or my supervision. We cried together and made a pact never to put each other in jeopardy again. We both were in agreement, that all we had in the world, was each other, and that we had to stick together.

But since Sean was on the warpath once again, now terrorizing my uncle in his workplace, I had no other choice but to take proactive measures to protect my family, to which end, I once again called his mother, Dawn, who lived in Florida in an attempt to get in touch with his brother, Hank. But although she was upset about what Sean had done, she refused to give me his brother's number, explaining that Hank had his own set of problems and that this might set him off in a way that might result in his violating his federal parole. But she did give me their sister, Colleen's number and promised me that, if she knew what was going on, she would intervene.

However, Unfortunately, my conversation with Colleen was brief and vague as, apparently intent on protecting her family, she made apologies for Sean, saying that he had been on a very rough road lately, and she wasn't exactly sure of what he was capable of doing. He was, she added, addicted to alcohol and heroin and had violent outbursts very regularly. She was worried for both my daughter and me. However, she would not divulge much more information regarding Sean. I ended the awkward conversation by thanking her for her help.

I was left in a state of confusion and fear of the unknown, once again trapped in Sean's world as I had been before. At that time, I could only hope that his mother, sister or brother would intercede and force him to stop holding my family hostage, a hope that seemed about to be realized when Hank called and told me the entire truth about Sean, including the fact that he had been in and out of rehabilitation treatment centers for drug and alcohol addiction, serving one particular stint imposed by the court due to an assault conviction after he had attacked a woman outside of a local convenience store. Sean had also flat-lined in at the hospital on two separate occasions due to an overdose of Xanax and alcohol. Hank went on to say that Sean lived in and out of crack houses in the South Bronx, having left his stroke disabled father following a beating, after which Hank had threatened to kill him if he ever did anything like that again.

Hank was serious about getting Sean placed in an institution for recovery for his addictions and proposed that, using Marie as bait, we might lure him into voluntarily getting professional help. He and his mother had previously tried to commit Sean but without success. But if I were to agree to this plan, he added, he would oversee everything. All verbal communication would also take place at Hank's appointed times. Marie's desire to connect with her father, the willingness of Sean to seek out a relationship, and Hank's orchestration of the plan seemed pretty foolproof. Before I hung up the phone, I told Hank I would give his plan very serious thought.

After thinking about our conversation at length, I decided that Hank's proposal had some merit, particularly since my only other option seemed to be to put my house on the market, quit my job and run away again. When I had escaped from Sean fourteen years earlier, I had taken only the belongings I could fit into the car. Aside from the trauma and fear, leaving him had been relatively uncomplicated. Now, with Hank, the only person who could control Sean, to protect us, we might be able to defuse a situation that might flare out of control again.

As a result, when Hank called me back the following week I agreed to meet him and his father for lunch in the Bronx, and bring Marie who had never met her family and would surely benefit from knowing more about her roots, particularly since she felt so abruptly rejected by Scott. But when she learned that the meeting would not include her paternal father, her smile faded. I didn't see it coming, the beginning of an entanglement, I would regret for all of my life.

EIGHT

Brother Intervenes

WHEN WE MET IN THE heart of downtown South Bronx, we decided, since it was in the middle of summer, to eat and then walk to the riverfront park. Hank and his father were pleasant and kept the meeting as light as possible.

As for Marie, she seemed happy to shine in the eyes of her new family. Sean's brother and father were kind and caring toward her, Hank reiterating that her father had some serious problems that had to be dealt with on a professional level. Marie listened to Hank lay out the plan to help Sean. He discussed all of the problems associated with his plans for Sean, stressing the importance of our cooperation. He explained that Sean needed to be supervised during phone conversations and future meetings and explained that Marie needed to refrain from calling him on her own because it was too dangerous.

It was obvious that Hank was the figure in control. His father was weak and unstable. Speaking with a crackle in his voice, he told me how many years prior to this day; he had been the one that answered the door for the sheriff's deputy, and that when I had filed for Marie's adoption, he had signed the legal documents, giving permission for her adoption to take place, letting the sheriff assume that he was Sean Donnelly. And since the deputy never asked him for his identification, he had allowed the assumption to stand uncorrected. He'd signed all of the documents for the adoption and no one knew the better. He said that we were better off far away from Sean and he thought that would help us remain distanced from him. That story answered many of my questions from the past, including why Sean had signed those papers so easily. At that time, Scott and I had assumed the worst would occur, so we took precautions and moved a few months later to another unlisted address, leaving me relieved that apparently, no action was to be taken to prevent our adoption plans. I had also thought that Sean was giving up trying to hunt us down, all of which had made our lives a lot easier back then.

Our afternoon with Hank and Marie's grandfather was bittersweet but far from the family reunion I had hoped it would be since Marie had previously only connected with Sean over the phone. When she expressed her disappointment to me on the ride home, my heart hurt to see the pain in her eyes, even though I attempted to cheer her up by reminding her that she would meet her father face to face at a later time when he recovered from his addictions and when it was safe. Her quest to discover her family roots was far from over.

After that family gathering, I knew that things were more complicated than I had anticipated. Hank's plan for a reunion between my daughter and his brother appeared to be a good tactical design in theory. However, when we combined the human equation and mixed it up with adolescence and drug addicted behaviors, it blew up in our faces and all but resulted in full-fledged war between the parties involved.

A few weeks after our meeting, Marie wanted to speak with her father. I had been in touch with Hank who had denied her request to have contact with him, based on his opinion that Sean would not commit to going away to a rehab for treatment but was dragging his feet instead of jumping at the opportunity for recovery. Ironically enough, Marie was angry at Hank who, as far as she was concerned, was keeping her father away from her. What she wanted was to meet her real dad, not a substitute uncle. She was determined to contact Sean and I knew that I had to intervene or our safety could be compromised.

Consequently, I called Sean for Marie and allowed her to speak with him if I supervised the phone call, that being the only way that I could be certain that Marie would not be tricked into divulging information about us. I couldn't ignore her pleas to speak with Sean, because I knew from past experience that, if I denied her request, she would sneak off and call him anyway. Now, with me part of the program, we planned on the different ways that we could help Sean recover from his addictions. It was an active participation on both our parts. Marie seemed so happy and had such hope for Sean's recovery. I was cautiously overseeing their conversations.

I placed the phone calls each time, pleased to find that Sean seemed to be calmer and less agitated, when he answered the phone, although sometimes he seemed confused, or slurred his words. But his threats had ceased, and he did sound very sincere in his desire to obtain help for his addictions, and to ultimately regain a relationship with his daughter. He even expressed a sincere sorrow for his inappropriate behavior in the past.

During those months his father's health had continued to falter and Sean often spoke of losing the only camaraderie he had ever had. Unfortunately, this prompted his focus on his daughter, and his desire to reunite with her, to concentrate on being the father he should have been. For a total of three months, Sean, Marie and I had in-depth phone conversations.

As time forged forward, I began to get a more empathic view of Sean. I saw a broken-down sorrowful soul, tormented by his past. It seemed to me that all of his addictions had chipped away at his body and his mind so that he was no longer the strong, turbulent man I had once known. As the days passed my desire to help Sean grew greater. Our daily communication took me on a slow path into a world I was not equipped to handle, one in which it was increasingly easy for me to be manipulated by him, one in which I actually came to believe that we could live happily ever after. Sean played on my love for my daughter who had a direct path to my heart. This other chord he struck was my desire to be loved.

Sean had talked about his father's illness with a heavy heart, convinced that his brother Hank wanted to lock him away in a treatment center, for the sole purpose of taking over his father's death benefits, despite the fact that their father had named Sean as the beneficiary. Hank and Colleen were to receive one dollar each while Sean was to receive the remainder of the insurance benefits, which amounted to approximately eighty thousand dollars. Sean explained that his father felt that both Hank and Colleen had been "traders" as he put it, because they accepted their stepfather into their lives. All of this had apparently given Sean motivation to get the treatment he needed as soon as his father recovered from his illness.

Marie had been dealt a bad hand of cards when it came to fathers, beginning with Sean and then being adopted by a man who had seemed to tossed her away, when she hit puberty, his solution in dealing with a rebellious teenager was to withdraw from her after telling her abruptly that she was not his child. Now I saw Sean's recovery as a way of restoring happiness to all of us.

Hank, on the other hand was irate. His plan for Sean's institutionalization took a spin into reverse when he saw that Sean had won my sympathy. "You are not equipped to deal with Sean's manipulation," he told me." He's gonna chew you up and spit you out into tiny pieces. Just never come running to me when he bashes your head in. You're stuck with it now. Deal with it. Don't call me, don't fuckin call me!"

He was convinced that Marie and I were thwarting his plans, for Sean's recovery, fully aware of just how naïve I was being. I can see now that his gruff interception was his way of protecting us. He was all too familiar with his brother's true nature. And by reminding me, over and over again that I was in over my head, he was trying to warn me. Hank was aware that we were about to traverse the road of destruction.

NINE

Daughter's Introduction to Paternal Father

MARIE HAD TO BE RUSHED to the local hospital by ambulance because of one of the severe asthma attacks she often had when exposed to seasonal allergies or intense stressful situations. During puberty, Marie had suffered terrible asthmatic reactions to her hormone imbalances, and now, as it became Indian summer, I was not surprised when the change in air quality, produced so much havoc in her lungs that she had to be rushed to the hospital.

As I entered the hospital room Marie looked like she had done something terribly wrong. As it turned out, Sean's mother, having been told of her asthma attack earlier that evening, had inadvertently shared the news with Sean who then began calling all of the Connecticut hospitals to find out where Marie had been admitted, and having finally found the right one, had, called Marie, establishing a contact I had feared over the past eleven months, since his attacked on my uncle.

Marie wanted to let him come see her at the hospital. She was so hopeful that she convinced me that seeing her father might help her. At least, it would help fill the hollow spot in her heart. At that point in time, I had been in communication with Sean for a few months and felt confident that he was willing to help himself without hurting us. Furthermore, I didn't think that the hospital was a bad place to allow them to meet. It was the sort of neutral territory in which I could call security if he acted inappropriately. And so Marie called him and he made plans to take the train in from the Bronx into Connecticut. I offered to pick him up at the Amtrak train station.

As I waited for him, my heart raced from my mixed emotions. I had expected to see an older man whose presence still demanded respect. Instead, what I saw, was a guy who hung his head down in shame and confusion, a sick and broken human being. He acted so out of touch with reality, that simple conversation was difficult and I felt an overwhelming sorrow wash over me. His clothing and body reeked with the aroma of smoke and alcohol but because I wanted, suddenly, so much to help him, I welcomed him warmly. It would be an invitation I would live to regret for all of my life. I opened Pandora's Box and there was no closing it from that day forth.

Sean was grateful for my kindness and he behaved himself perfectly during the entire ride to and from the hospital. Tears streaming down her cheeks, Marie was in shock when she saw him. What neither of us realized was that he behaved in such a disassociated way because drugs and alcohol had permanently disoriented him.

Sean was spinning in a fog like state of chemical confusion but Marie didn't notice nor do I think she knew why he was acting the way he was. This was her moment to shine. He told her how he had looked for her for many years. He told her that his family had refused to help him find her over the years, but that he had never given up. My heart ached for my little girl's pain and hurt. She cried that she wanted to help him and make him well and he agreed that he was in dire need of help for his addictions. He made promises to the both of us that seemed so sincere that we both were sold on the idea of helping him recover. I wanted to fix this broken down man, for my daughter and for myself. In my mind, it seemed that our existence depended upon mending all that was broken in Sean.

And so Sean was invited into our lives, just as he had hoped he would be. We began our relationship based on the agreement that he would cooperate in his own recovery. My home was extended to him on a temporary basis until he was accepted into a treatment center. Marie seemed delighted to have him with us and to participate in his recovery, as well. He agreed to the set conditions and he agreed that he required professional help. He was grateful for the help and he seemed appreciative for the free fresh start.

We had begun our journey toward a whole family unit. It had some bumps and pitfalls, but we were sure that we would overcome them together, one step at a time. This was my vision for us. I spent all of my spare hours dedicating my time and attention to Sean's recovery. For a period of eight weeks, I was completely consumed by my involvement in his healing. I contacted professional treatment centers, drug and alcohol counseling and determined that the process was more involved than I had imagined. I spoke to every center in the Connecticut and New York area only to discover that there were differences between inpatient and outpatient therapy along with the different requirements and guidelines for each one until it seemed that my life consisted of making appointments for acceptance interviews for many different programs. I traveled mostly to the Bronx for ophthalmologist and regular physicians appointments and since Sean was on public assistance in New York, he had to go pick his checks up there, as well. I traveled from the State Welfare Office to the Federal Social Security Office, for Sean to gather his life together. It seemed that we were constantly driving over to New York for something related to his needs.

We met in the city with his mother, Dawn, and went from outpatient centers filling out applications for acceptance. Since Sean had experienced medical problems that involved renal failure, he was rejected by two of the facilities. As Sean's mother explained it to me, she had flown in from Florida to save her son from drug overdose after Hank had called her and told her that Sean had manipulated me into taking him in, and that he was no longer able to control Sean's addictions. She would have to fly in and try and save him herself because Hank had given up the fight. She said that if Sean died from an overdose, she would never forgive herself for not having done all she could do to help him. She also let me know that she was tired of feeling guilty for running away from his abusive father. She believed that Sean had never forgiven her for leaving them and he would never accept her new husband.

Dawn admitted that it was Sean that made her move all the way to Florida. She, like me, had had to get away from him in order to start a new life, her decision being prompted by an incident that occurred in her home when Sean, while visiting, had threatened at gunpoint her husband who had just been recovering from heart surgery. After that, they sold their house and moved out of the state, but she had never been able to escape the guilt she felt for Sean's hatred of women, a hatred which stemmed from her abandonment of him. She apologized for all of the times Sean had beaten me in the past and told me that Sean's father was a "mean man" whom she had left because she could no longer stand it.

When she asked me why I was helping Sean now, I told her that I had been unable to achieve happiness in relationships my whole life. I shared with her a brief version of my marriage to Scott and the reasons for our breakup, including our fast paced life involving drug usage. I told her that I understood Sean's need to be loved and how he filled that missing void with drugs and alcohol, just as I had filled my life with men who were incapable of loving me. I also reminded her of the fact that Marie wanted her father. I felt that no other man was going to love Marie as her own biological father would love her, and I explained how perfect it was for all three of us to reunite for a greater purpose of developing into a whole unit. And because she too understood exactly where I was coming from, I let her know that Marie and I wanted to bring her son back, from the "mad world" in which he presently resided.

Now, however, the dispute with Hank took center stage. Hank wanted Sean admitted to an in-house treatment program. Having strategically cut off his brother's access to drugs on the street in their neighborhood, and taken away his connection to prescription drugs provided by the local doctors and pharmacies, he had had Sean backed into a corner, until I became his only avenue of escape. Hank was pretty upset with me for becoming Sean's way out, all of which led to a violent confrontation between them, after which Hank threw up his hands and left to return to the South Bronx.

From that moment on, nearly all of my time when I was not working was dedicated to Sean's physical requirements. I fed him, made sure he showered, shaved and stayed away from alcohol. I took care of his skin, which was covered with acne, with facials and back mask therapy, cut his hair and made sure he had clean clothes to wear, as well as making certain that he took his anti-anxiety pills and the medication that prevented seizures which could be brought on from alcohol withdrawal because of which he could do little for himself, including daily showering, eating and brushing his teeth. He was unable to do much of anything without my help other than chain smoke cigarettes.

On a more positive note, both Marie and I came to know him better as we learned about what had happened to him in those missing years. As it turned out, Sean had been married and divorced to a girl who moved to California, and had a five year old son. He also had an illegitimate daughter who lived somewhere in Connecticut. Over the years, he and his father had moved from the house in Stamford into a row home in the Bronx. Sean spoke of the streets of the South Bronx as if he was in some kind of a special club, calling them "The Jungle". He swore that he was in the Irish mob and that he fought wars against the Italians in those streets. He told me his brother had been a trader which meant that he sold drugs to the Irish, and that he was glad when he was finally caught and sent to jail. And although he himself had held a few odd jobs painting houses, he was now collecting city welfare, although he intended to start working again, as soon as, he conquered his addictions.

That was where Marie and I came in to help him overcome his drug and alcohol problem. But our plans, which started out as being extremely promising, ended up tragically hopeless, primarily because he was using us to get rid of Hank and enable him to return to his addictions despite the fact that both Marie and I only wanted to help save him from chemical deterioration and self-destruction. Sean needed to use that willingness to help his own agenda. It was a perfect set up for Sean to continue his lifestyle of chemical check out.

Everything was perfect for his plan to succeed. My house was far enough away from his brother's control that he could do as he pleased without Hank there to stop him. Once Sean had worked his way into our lives, he would then control us, and continue his old patterns of living. Our objections would not matter and would not hold any weight, unlike his brother's constraints, which had squeezed off all of Sean's connections.

To say that I was forced to comply was an understatement. After six weeks of being completely exhausted, I had very little energy left in me to keep up the hectic pace. I was so run down that it weakened my resolve, and distracted my focus from our set goal. I had too many other factors, distractions and diversions, to set my sight on one thing at a time. And the longer I cared for and nurtured Sean, the healthier and stronger he became until finally he began to object to any sort of control, his number one objection being any sort of rehabilitation program. I became accustomed to hearing him offer one excuse after another, including his father's health and the fact that he didn't need any more help than he was getting to recover, not to receive treatment.

All of a sudden his attitude toward me changed from being grateful to resentful. He accused me of being in cahoots with his brother Hank as well as of planning to force him to go into an institution just like his brother had tried to do. In Sean's eyes, I too was becoming the enemy. He was quickly focusing on all of my faults, in order to avoid his responsibilities for his own recovery as he pressured me to accept his ideas. In other words, the old Sean was quickly emerging, as he began his journey back to malevolence. He was on a straight path to darkness.

Sean had me running at full speed, on my days off and after working hours. Since my days consisted of eleven hours of standing on my feet, I was exhausted at the day's end, particularly since I was always worried about what Sean was doing at the house. He was drinking again, and I also suspected that he was using drugs. He constantly scratched his arms, back and nose as if bugs were crawling on him and would scratch his skin until he drew blood. He would sit, Indian style and chain-smoked cigarettes, even at night, once burning a hole the size of an orange, in one of my blankets. Not only would he sneak out to the liquor store, during the day to consume alcohol, but also he would polish off a case of beer in an afternoon. He was rapidly becoming a mean-spirited drunk who craved heroin. Sean had me drive him into the city to pick up his check, after which he would make an excuse to stop at his so-called friend's house, saying that he owed him money. He would make me wait in the car for him, while he bought his drugs. Of course, when I asked questions he would lie and become defensive. I usually dropped the inquiries because I didn't want to push him into a rage.

Not that it took much to make him angry. When one of the boys who was part of Marie's circle said something offhand that annoyed him, he had to be restrained from beating him up and once, in a convenience store, he attacked a clerk for "coming on" to me.

His opinions were affecting Marie on a very basic level. When, he said she had become a Donnelly again, he insisted that her friends not be allowed in the house, especially not in her bedroom, nor would she be running around all over town looking like a floozy in revealing garments.

He didn't feel that Marie was totally his to own to boss around, until her name was changed from that Jew bastard's name back to Donnelly. He went so far as to speak of Marie as a young piece of meat that he was going to hook up with some city hoodlums, although in the next breath he might accuse her of wearing clothing that was too revealing. That was how erratic his thoughts had become.

One night he told me that Marie was laughing at him. He was convinced that I had turned her against him, and that she was mocking him, in front of her friends. Sean was becoming his old self again, right before my eyes. He often accused me of thinking I was better than he. One night he walked around my house pointing to different pieces of furniture and saying, "Oh you with your fancy life in your fancy house. You think you're better than me, but you're just like my mother with your fancy little nose in the air, I'll show you how hard you can fall, I'll watch all your snob hob things disappear and that'll fix you. You think you're better than me, don't ya!" His ranting didn't require an answer, but I often I felt compelled to verbally defend myself.

Meanwhile, Marie was spending less and less time at home. She and I became more distant. She wanted to have either me or her father to herself. The happy little fairytale family was quickly becoming a nightmare. She was already in her rebellious teenage hormone-induced stage which, combined with the Sean arrangement, was a bad mix. Consequently, we argued and disagreed more so than ever. Sean enjoyed the discord between us and encouraged Marie to give me a hard time. He would provoke her to start an argument with me which often would escalate into a full-blown screaming match. One night he encouraged Marie to drive the car and when she was picked up by the police for speeding, he woke me to say proudly that she was just like her father.

Marie was out to give me a hard time, which came very easy with her father around. Sean would ask Marie questions about me and other men during the fourteen years of his absence, and then, when he and I were alone together, would accuse me of being a slut. At one point I begged Marie not to tell him anything about me, although I did not explain, as I probably should have, that he was using what she said against me. Anyway, the result of all this was that we grew further and further apart. In order to protect Marie, I encouraged her to stay out and over her friend's house as much as possible. I could see Sean was reverting to the scary character he had once been and knew that it was just a matter of time before he totally flipped out. I didn't want Marie to witness that.

In mid-November 1993, Colleen called my house to say that their father had been admitted into Saint Ann's hospital in the Bronx for liver complications and that his prognosis didn't look good, particularly since, although he was only in his fifties, he was already very frail. He was, like Sean, an alcoholic and the many years of drinking had taken a toll on his body.

Sean took such a turn for the worst with the news of his father's illness that any question of drug and alcohol treatment was out of the question. I had all I could do to help Sean cope with his father's illness, and could only hope that he would go get help for his addictions. But, of course, the reality of the matter was that Sean had no intention of recovery, not before his father became ill or after. Sean had worked his way back into my life, and he had quickly taken over. Now Sean was at the helm of the ship.

TEN

Caustic Reunion

My life now took a rapid turn into total chaos. It was near the holiday and emotions were running high. The pressure of Sean's father's illness took a toll on us all. Sean was becoming more depressed and erratic in his moods, and, as usual, drinking heavily, often saying that he would have nothing to live for if his father died, conveniently ignoring the fact that his brother, sister and I were heavily committed to his recovery. But he felt he would be totally alone in the world of course, having spent most of his lifetime living with his father. Even when he was married, his father had shared the same residence, and more recently, when he had moved into my house, he was usually so high that he didn't know where he was. Now he couldn't deal with the fact that his father was incapable of taking care of them anymore. He often claimed that his father was his best friend and that he had provided him with the only real security that he had ever known, ignoring the fact that they had survived by feeding off of one another. Their "thicker than thieves" relationship was oddly twisted out of a warped sense of allegiance and dedication to each other. Now that his mental capacity was on overload, Sean feared the unknown lifestyle he was about to embark upon, and it affected his ability to control his rage.

Sean's mood swings became more frequent as he began to concentrate on all the things that had to be done. And if they were not done immediately, he would go into a panic mode. If we had an appointment at two o'clock, we had to be there hours before or he would not stop mumbling on about it. When we had to go into the Bronx a few times to pick up Sean's things at his friend's house, he put on a show of belligerence toward me. The visit ended when he swung a wet rubber mat and hit me with it on the side of my face. When I ran out of the house to my car and pulled away, he dashed to stand in front of the car, forcing me to swerve around him in order to hightail it back to Connecticut. At that point, I should have never looked back, but of course, when he called and apologized, playing the "My father is dying" card I agreed to pick him up the next day.

Trips to the city were always filled with surprises. When I drove into the Bronx again the next evening, I took along one of Marie's older girlfriends that lived around the corner from us, thinking that she would be company for me. Kerri and I listened to music on the way to the city to pick up Sean and all seemed well when we arrived at Sean's friends' house, and I beeped the horn. When Sean came out, carrying green plastic bags which he put in the trunk, he told me that he had to go back to collect some money from a friend who owed him and that he would only be a few minutes.

All of a sudden this blonde haired guy dressed in torn pants and an army jacket came walking down the street toward my car, and when Sean looked up and started yelling, demanding to know where his money was, the fellow set off running with Sean in pursuit. As Kerri and I watched in horror, Sean caught him and began beating him furiously. Knocking him down on the curb, he continued to strike him with his fist and feet, and when he was done punching his bloody face, he kicked his body until the man no longer moved.

When Sean had finished bludgeoning this man, he ran back to the car and got in, shouting at me to drive off. The entire ride home he went on about how this punk had stolen money from him, and how lucky he was that he hadn't killed him. As it turned out the man owed Sean money from the Xanax he had fronted him. That was when I found out for sure that Sean was selling prescription drugs on the city streets for extra money. This was my reintroduction to Sean's violent behaviors in full color. Kerri and I were silent the entire ride back to Connecticut. I was beginning to realize that I had created quite a predicament for us, by allowing this man back into our lives.

My premonition that Sean's violence would soon spill over on me was about to become a reality. On Thanksgiving eve and I spent the entire day working. After a grueling eleven hour grueling workday, I drove home to prepare for the next days' holiday dinner. It was to be our first holiday spent together as a family and I wanted it to be special. I had gone shopping for all of the special foods to make it memorable. All I had to do was to get everything ready to cook in the morning. But when I opened the front door, I was taken by surprise when Sean came charging at me, yelling something about my boyfriend having called me.

He was like a madman, his eyes black and empty as he punched me around the room, ignoring my attempts to calm him down. Blood pouring down my face, I managed to crawl up the stairs to my bedroom where there was a deadlock on the door and a panic button that would alert the police. By the time the police arrived, Sean had broken in the panels of my door and while they subdued him with the help of a trained police German shepherd, I was sobbing with relief.

The police took me down to the Darien station house, and while Sean was being interrogated in the room next to me, I told two of the officers all about Sean's heroin and alcohol addictions, his abusive assaults in detail, along with the fact that he had a fake driver's license in his brother's name. I informed them of his history of selling prescription pills on the city streets and reminded them of his attacks on my family in the past. Their response was to call the Fairfield County Judge to request a temporary restraining order. Once that order was in place I was encouraged to return home. I begged the officer to hold him overnight until he sobered up. I pleaded with them to transfer him to a drug treatment center, if they decided not to hold him there at the station, but received no reassurances.

An hour later, after I had driven home, I was startled by a knock at the door. It was the local police Officer, Percy Packs, who told me that Sean was being released from the station and he needed money for a taxicab to return to the Bronx. I was astounded by this news. I couldn't believe that the police were releasing him directly after having dragged him out of my house, high on alcohol and heroin. Yet the police released him from their custody after midnight, and actually had the gall to send someone to get money for cab fare for a man who tried to seriously hurt me! This was a moment of awakening for me. I could no longer believe that the police would protect me.

As it turned out, I was right to feel terrorized since Sean used the money I sent him to take a cab, not to the Bronx, but to my house, the restraining order in his pocket. Once again, I called 911 and Sean was arrested for the second time in one night. He was transferred to the Fairfield County Jail where he remained for the Thanksgiving holiday.

The next day was Thanksgiving Day. I cried the entire day, for so many reasons. This was supposed to be a day to be thankful to have an abundance of gratefulness for the many blessings bestowed upon you but I could only be grateful to be alive. At the same time, particularly after speaking to Colleen on the phone and listening to her express her sadness that Sean would be celebrating the holiday in a cold jail cell, I was engulfed in guilt. As usual the emphasis was on "poor Sean," and in the end, after a phone call in which he expressed regret, I provided bail.

That was one of the monumental moments for us. From that day forward my life took on a whole new twist of distortion with the introduction of an attorney who had represented Sean in a case of assault on a woman a few years prior. The judge had reduced a jail sentence to mandatory rehabilitation treatment imposed by the court. This time, Sean gave a heavily edited account of what had happened and tried to convince Mr. Schull that I had panicked and called the police for no reason. I listened to Sean tell his attorney that he only used an open hand while striking me. Clearly Sean was obsessed with the worry of a possible prison term and once again I submitted, against my better judgment, and made an appointment with the lawyer about dropping the restraining order. Two days later, I appeared before the Fairfield County Superior Court and told the judge I no longer wished to have the restraining order lodged against him.

From that point on my life was similar to a roller coaster ride without the thrill. Sean became a time bomb. His abusive outburst occurred on a daily basis. The escalation of violence grew to extreme proportions. Each day that passed made me wonder, what will happen tomorrow, and how will I survive it?

I worked four ten hours days a week, and in between those days, I crammed in all of Sean's errands. His father's health was failing and it was just a matter of time before he expired. We spent many hours in and out of the hospital. One of those days, I allowed Sean to take my car to do his other errands while I remained at the hospital with his father, shaping up his dad's hair and making him more presentable. Sean arrived back at the hospital four hours late, the smell of alcohol permeating the room when he entered. He was so intoxicated that he couldn't walk a straight line, and I could see from that all-too-familiar look in his eyes that he was daring me to say anything to him about being hours late in returning to the hospital, not to mention his intoxication.

Living with Sean now was like listening to a tune without a variation. After the next trip to the hospital, Sean made me stop in this small row home so he could pay back money he owed to a friend. That's the story he told me anyway, but when he returned to the car, he seemed different, almost strangely calm and I could see that he had shot up a fix of heroin. And he had courted danger since we both could have been arrested and worse still, shot by one of the street thugs. Sean got a kick out of being on the streets. He said," All of the street Niggers respect me, cause they know I'm fucking crazy. No one fucks with me." After that experience I was too tired and scared to run Sean into the city again. He lied so much that I couldn't trust anything he said. It was enough to come home from working ten hours to figure out if it was safe to enter the house. His alcohol consumption, coupled with his father dying, pending assault charges and pressure from his family to rehabilitate his addictions, sent Sean over the edge.

The hospital runs from Connecticut to the South Bronx were so frequent that I finally gave Sean my car to drive himself. I had to work and function in a manner that might appear to be semi normal. People around me were beginning to notice the change in me. I no longer had a bubbly demeanor. It was all I could do to gather the strength to make it through another day. Sean on the other hand had been nursed back to health again and was no longer the broken individual I had seen when he had returned. Because I had nurtured him, fed him and cared for him, he had become a more dangerous person, while I was once more broken in spirit.

Sean had a special liking to a game of questions and answers when we were having sex, asking me how many men I had been with or, as he put it, "fucked," during the fourteen years we had been apart. And if I hesitated, he began tormenting me, twisting my arm and threatening me so that I could no longer make a living, claiming that I needed to be knocked down a few rungs on the ladder. Again and again, he compared me to his mother.

His comparison was made with much disdain and contempt. He wanted to bring me down to his level, as he put it.

Once he hurt me so badly, throwing me to the floor, that I visited my family doctor, Dr. Vera Mathews who, seeing the bruises, asked me what had happened, and had no choice but to accept my explanation that it had happened when I fell off a ladder while trying to change a light bulb. After treating me and prescribing painkillers for the pain, Doctor Mathews told me if I needed to talk or if I had any questions she would be available, for me at her emergency number.

This was the beginning of the bedroom incidents during which Sean prided himself on inflicting pain on me. What started out as emotional harassment soon turned to sodomy and rape, while he, increasingly comparing his physical attributes to those of "that Jew" Scott, while denying that he had any homosexual tendencies by saying that he didn't like fucking assholes. I learned early on that it was best not to comment on anything Sean said and gave very little input to any of his grandiose statements. I cautiously answered questions that were posed to me, aware as I was of his need for an immediate response. My comments were limited to a less than few words. Sometimes it infuriated Sean and other times it saved me from further interrogation and punishment.

Sean had a great appreciation for the acquired power over me in the bedroom, clearly enjoying the fact that there I was at his mercy. He would touch my nipples and then squeeze and twist them until I screamed in agony. Other times, he would begin to feel my vagina and declared that he could tell that I had had sex with someone else that day, and that I must have fucked someone during my lunch break, reinforcing his accusations by shoving his entire hand up inside me. When I would beg him to leave me be, he would laugh and tell me what a whore I was. My only consolation was the hope that once the stress of his father's illness was over, he would become a normal person again.

Marie called me at work on a Saturday to tell me that, although it was only eleven o'clock in the morning, Sean had already finished drinking a half a case of beer. It seemed that Marie had had a girlfriend sleep over and while they were making breakfast, Sean began staggering through the house in his underwear, mumbling under his breath and giving Marie and her girlfriend threatening looks.

"He asked us what we were looking at," Marie told me, "And then that he could drink if he wanted to because his father was dying. "And now he's been following me around, abusing me," she added. "What am I supposed to do?"

She was getting her first taste of the dark side of her biological father who, that morning, grabbed her by the arm, squeezing it tight enough for her to know he meant business. When she begged me to come home and do something with him. I told her to get dressed and leave the house with her girlfriend immediately. This incident turned on the light switch of reality for me, serving as a moment of true clarity. My life had spun out of control. I didn't know how to ground myself back to normalcy.

Just as I had expected, Sean was in rare form when I returned home, accusing me of turning his daughter against him and he even bragged about how smart he was and how dumb I was to have fallen for his lies, telling me that he would break me. I was subjected to what seemed to be an endless explosion of ferocious rhetoric until Sean eventually required an alcoholic beverage, both to soothe his dry throat and to ease his frantic mind, after which I was finally released from being the sole participant in his captive audience.

By early December1993, Sean's father was in the intensive care unit, being kept alive with the help of life support machines and Sean was in full throttle, overwhelmed by dread. He insisted that it was imperative for him to be present at the hospital during my working hours. Sean often spoke of suicide and killing the people he hated most when his father died. He would tell me that, when his father died, he wouldn't have anything to live for, all of which I found extremely alarming because his thoughts came about randomly, sputtered out in fragmented phases. I continued to allow him to use the car even though I was fully aware that Sean had a few license revocations due to DWI's and DUI's. He had a valid Connecticut state driver's license, which he obtained under his brother's name. I didn't want to deny him at such a delicate time, because I was convinced that he would go over the edge.

Early the next morning, Sean and I drove to the salon where I faced an eleven-hour workday with one arm in a sling, my only hope being, as he drove away, that he would appreciate my kindness and respect the great privilege that had been given to him and that he would be on time to pick me up at eight-thirty that night. But when that time came and went, and he did not appear, I began to feel queasiness in the pit of my stomach. It was an evening that started with misty rain and quickly developed into a wintry mix because of falling temperatures. I waited inside a convenience store until I could no longer stand it and began to keep going outside into the blistery cold in order to look down the road in anticipation of my ride. I shuffled in and out of the store, until I was completely soaked. Time progressed and still there wasn't any sign of Sean with my car.

It was ten-thirty when Sean finally turned into the driveway of the store parking lot, maneuvering the car was with obvious uncertainty. When the power window receded into the door. I came face to face with Sean's brazen smirk. He was extremely inebriated and ready for an argument, defensive for showing up over two hours late, and claimed that it was because I had pressured him that he had smashed the car bumper. As usual, he disassociated his responsibility for any of the events during that day or evening, and if I protested, viewed it as another attack of his person, just one more conspiracy to bring him down. His method of defense was to stamp us all out.

On December 10, 1993, Sean insisted that I drive him to the city after work, unwilling to face the fact that the evening's weather was dangerously wet with sleet forecast. Despite my best efforts to be agreeable, the usual accusations followed until finally, in a rage, he began to strike me. In order to avoid an accident, I turned off to the side of the road and getting out of the car, ran as fast as my legs could carry me, to the nearest building, an Asian restaurant, with Sean at my heels, shouting threats. I barricaded myself in the public bathroom, after calling out to two men, who were standing outside, to call the police.

I waited for what seemed a long time before I timidly came out from the lavatory area only to find Sean pacing outside. And although I asked the man at the desk to call the police, he refused and insisted that I should leave the restaurant, forcing me to call them myself from the pay phone in the lobby, all the time watching Sean pacing outside. I was, of course, aware of the ramifications of Sean's pending arrest with his father so near death. But what could I do? When the squad car arrived, I refused to press charges, with the result that they drove him to Colleen's house and I drove home, my heart pounding, more aware than ever before that, because of Sean, my life was spiraling out of control.

Less than a week later, when Sean's father passed away, Sean took a dramatic turn for the worse. Completely losing his bearings, he fell into a deep dark abyss filled with lawlessness, continuing as usual to threaten the pending death of himself, his brother and myself. Clearly Sean was set on a course of doom and dread. He stated that he had no reason to go on living and that he would take his brother and me down with him. It was terrible to watch Sean sink deeper into drug and alcohol abuse in order to escape reality.

ELEVEN

War Is Waged

SEAN HAD WAGED WAR AGAINST humanity. Even though his father had been incapacitated, he still had remained Sean's mental anchor and now without him, Sean seemed determined to continue on a course of utter destruction. Clearly having been sent over the edge, he became more dangerous than ever.

On December 19, 1993, Sean's behavior spiraled completely out of control. He had been drinking in an attempt to drown out his sorrows, but instead intoxication allowed him to act out his fears in the form of aggression. Funeral preparations for his father had to be made that day with Colleen insisting that Sean be present to discuss the financial obligations, particularly since he was the only beneficiary of their father's insurance policy, except for the one dollar he had left her and Hank, a position he had been forced into when Sean had convinced him that she and Hank were traitors because they had accepted their stepfather into the family. Now his signature was needed. She also needed Sean to grant permission for the undertaker to proceed with their father's funeral preparations.

Sean drank the entire time we spent at Colleen's house. He kept sending her children into the kitchen to bring him more beer and, as a consequence, the conversation became more aggressive when the pressure was put on Sean regarding the fair distribution of the monies. He kept telling Colleen that she could have a substantial sum, but that his brother Hank was only getting a dollar. After all, Sean said, that was exactly how their "pops" had wanted it to be, as he repeated, over and over again, that Hank was not getting a "fuckin dime" of his money.

The longer we remained at his sister's house, the more Sean became intoxicated. When I tried to stop his nephew from getting him the seventh bottle of beer, Sean demanded, that I shut the fuck up, and mind my own business. He continued to argue with Colleen over their father's funeral arrangements until he finally agreed to allow her to take care of all of the communication with the funeral director. He signed the documents that allowed the director to take the cost of the funeral out of the insurance check, whenever it arrived, and told Colleen to have the check come to her house so that he could pick it up and split it with her with the condition that Colleen didn't give Hank any of the money on the basis that it had been his fault that he, Sean, was no longer given access to "the jungle". She agreed with anything Sean told her to appease him since otherwise, she would not have been able to bury their father. Sean held the power over them for a change. He was enjoying this moment very much.

"You and my fucking brother are going to pay big time, for fucking me out of my life," he told me when we left Colleens. "I was just fine in the jungle until Hank had to be the "Five 0" and squeeze the fuckin life out of me. You're right in there too, you fuckin cunt! You both will pay! And don't you fuckin forget it"!

I drove to the Chuck's restaurant and went along with anything Sean suggested in the hopes that he would calm down, but even when we were seated and had ordered, he continued his rant.

"You think I can't eat out at a fancy restaurant bitch?" he announced. "I'll show you, Ms. High and Mighty. You think you're better than me don't you, whore? You'll see how good you are when I break you down, bitch. Look. I can hold my fuckin' fork right. I should stab you right in the fuckin' hand with it."

And taking my hand, he picked up the steak knife and stabbed my palm with it. Sobbing, I jumped up from the table and ran out of the front door of the restaurant, but by the time I open my car door, Sean had me by the back of my hair. He demanded that I get in the car and drive him to the Amtrak train station, so that he could go into the city, saying that he wanted to be around his friends and grieve his father's death. He wanted to get away from me, the "miserable bitch!"

His request was a gift from heaven to my ears. I knew that if I could get him to the Bronx that I would have time to try to figure out a plan of escape. And so I agreed to take him to the Amtrak train station in Stamford. But on the way there, he changed his mind and decided to go home with me, and when, thinking of Marie and my safety, I tried to dissuade him, he fell into a fury.

"Drive to your house, bitch!" he shouted. "I just told you to take me to Darien, you fuckin' cunt. I know what you're up to. You've got plans for later and you're trying to get rid of me out of state. Now take me to your house before I fuckin' kill you right now, on this fuckin' road!"

Sean was out of his mind with anger and rage and became more enraged when I pulled up at the entrance to the Amtrak train station. I begged him to get on a train and go to the city to be with his friends, but there was no way I could reason with him. Sean was at a level of rage that I had never witnessed before. I knew that my life depended on my ability to escape him.

To that end, I stepped on the gas petal, flooring it while locking the steering wheel and forcing the car to go around in a continual circle. In my desperation, I could only hope to make him dizzy enough for me to get out of that car and run to safety which, after a few minutes, I did, running toward the highway with Sean at my heels swearing and swinging a metal bar that was an anti-theft lock, all the time threatening to kill me. Finally he came close enough to strike me on the back of my head, and when I finally fell to the ground, proceeded to drag me back to the car where, cursing, he pushed me into the back seat of the car.

"That's the last time you'll run from me, bitch," he shouted, getting behind the wheel, "You're finished. I'm taking you somewhere and finishing you off. You're going far out in the middle of nowhere, bitch. Nobody will find your body for a long fuckin' time. I'll make sure of it. You're dead, you cunt!"

I knew he was not making idle threats. He was going to kill me as soon as the car stopped, and in my panic, I found myself reaching for the package containing a letter opener that I had received from a client as a Christmas gift and thought, seriously of stabbing him in the back of the neck. But because I knew that if I did not kill him instantly, he would kill me, I grabbed a plastic bag instead and throwing it over his head, pushed the automatic window button. While Sean tore at the bag as it tightened over his head, slowing the car in the process, I leaped out, and threw myself against a car that had stopped for a red light, crying, "Help me, please! Someone help me, please! He's trying to kill me!" And when the driver did not respond, I threw myself in the passenger seat and cried, "Go! Drive fast, please! He'll kill me! I don't care where you take me, just please drive!" Meanwhile, Sean was standing in the middle of the intersection yelling, "She's crazy! Don't believe anything she says. She's crazy, really crazy."

Fortunately the stranger apparently did not believe him because, at my request, he took me to the Stamford police station, and a police officer escorted me into a cubical area where I remained for several hours filing a police report explaining the accounts of the evening's life threatening situations. I also recounted my past history of abuse inflicted by Sean, including his most recent arrest, re-arrest and restraining order. The officer made several telephone calls to other police departments of other jurisdictions, and then informed me that a police car would arrive shortly to take me to the Darien police department in Connecticut.

By the time the squad car arrived, I was in hysterics. Was there no end to this show of bureaucracy! After filing another report, I was taken to the Amtrak Station Police, to file another complaint, because that was where the incident took place. It was my third criminal complaint against Sean that evening.

I was then taken to the Amtrak train station parking lot where I found my car abandoned in the lot. Outside, to the rear of the trunk on the ground, laid the metal club that Sean used to assault me earlier that evening. My car doors were both unlocked but the keys were not anywhere to be found, and so, unbelievable as it sounds, I was then informed that my car would have to be impounded, as evidence, and that I would be able to retrieve it the following day. It was assumed that Sean had taken the Amtrak train to the Bronx which was out of the State of Connecticut's jurisdiction. The authorities told me that they could not help me arrest Sean if he, in fact, had fled to another state. They ask if I had anyone who could pick me up.

Knowing that I couldn't go home because I wasn't sure if Sean was waiting for me there, I called my friends Phil and Denise Kenny to come get me at the Darien police station. In a letter written subsequently, Denise described the scene as follows:

"My husband and I ran to pick her up in a hurry. When we arrived at the station, she was propped up as if she were a rag doll . . . My husband and I were shocked at the sight of her. She had no makeup on her face, which revealed many bruises. Her jeans were torn at the knees and dirty. She had dried blood on her hands . . . My husband had to carry her to our car, because she couldn't bend her knees to walk . . . When we brought her back to our home, she proceeded to explain to us that all of her bruises were the result of Sean's attacks. She said he became extremely violent with her, telling her that he should have killed her a long time ago. He told her that he was going to take her to some remote place where no one would ever find her."

Phil and Denise drove me back to their house and helped me clean my wounds, after which I called Marie who was at a girlfriend's and told her not to go home under any circumstances. Once again I borrowed the firearm for protection. After that I made an appointment to see Dr. Matthews the next day, and because the anti-anxiety pills she gave me were not enough, I called a physician I had seen years before and managed to double the prescription.

A few days passed before I conjured up the courage to drive home to pick up clothes and get money out of my safety deposit box. Being in that empty house alone caused me enormous anxiety and fear of Sean's reprisal. At that moment, realizing that I couldn't stay there in my house, I decided to make a desperate plead for help from Sean's brother Hank. The last time we spoke Hank had been furious about my intervention in his plan for his brother's recovery and had specifically informed me that I was on my own. He further instructed me not to call him when Sean chewed me up and spat me out, as he phrased it. Now, however, I swallowed deeply and pushed the number on my phone's hand piece.

As it turned out, Hank had expected to receive a similar phone call from me, regarding this subject. He had an "I told you so attitude" which was mixed with a little touch of sarcasm, and didn't hesitate to let me know that I made a fine mess out of the situation. He told me in no uncertain terms that if he were to intervene, things would have to be done his way, including taking possession of all of Sean's legal and medical information that I had. I agreed to any condition that Hank set forth just as long as he was willing to protect me, and paced about nervously until he arrived.

Hank gathered up all of Sean's documents that I held in my safe, including his fake social security number, Connecticut driver's license issued in Hank's name, arrest complaint for assault against me, original restraining order, eye doctor receipts, family doctor's receipts and the list of medications he had been prescribed. Hank told me that Sean had flat-lined a couple of times in the Bronx hospitals due to an overdose of a Xanax, heroin and alcohol combination, after which Hank had dragged him out of crack houses and abandoned buildings where drug addicts gathered to ride out their highs. He had been closing in on Sean when I came into the picture and prevented him from being forced to recover, but he had known that it was only a matter of time before I was crushed into submission.

That was, I told him, putting it mildly. I was a cracked shell of a person, running for my life. Hank was the closest thing to a fortress that I could think of. He was the only individual that Sean had ever feared, and now I turned to him as my savior, still so rattled that I was drinking, and consuming nerve pills at a rate of triple the dose. Even though I was chemically influenced it was the first time I could remember I felt safe. Hank's house was the key to shelter and security, from Sean's angry rage.

Hank made a few phone calls trying to find out where Sean was hiding out. Finally, around midnight, Sean contacted his brother by phone and I could hear him threatening to kill Hank. He told him that he knew I was hiding out there. Sean accused us of having an illicit affair and promised to kill us both.

When Hank hung up the phone, I was so shaken that I had taken out the pistol from my luggage which enraged Hank because he was on Federal parole, and a firearm was a violation of his parole conditions. Taking it away from me, he assured me that I would be safe with him, at that moment I broke down, tears streamed down my cheeks and pooling on the front of my shirt.

When the morning sun rose and peeked through the living room blinds, I awoke to find a note from Hank explaining that he had left to do errands. His phone kept ringing and ringing but I dared not answer it. Instead I ran upstairs and hid in the front bedroom until I heard the front door open and I heard Hank's voice. The messages Sean had left on his phone were chilling, ranging as they did from, "Go fuck Margo up the ass," to "Get ready, cock suckers cause I'm coming to kill ya both!"

A few hours later a car pulled up the narrow city street and idled in front of Hank's house and one of the two men inside honked the horn. Then, as Hank went outside, the door opened and Sean appeared, calling, "Margo, come on out here. I promise I won't hurt you hon. Come on out and come with me, I'm not going to hurt you. I just want you to leave Hank's house. Come on, I love you Margo. I need you right now, Margo. You have to help me. My father is dead. I'm sorry I hurt you. I won't hurt you again, Come on with me."

"Get the fuck out of here, Sean," Hank demanded, standing on the front step. "She is not going anywhere with you. You're a fucking mess, and she is not leaving this house with you or going anywhere near you. Go the fuck back to the jungle where you belong."

At that, Sean suddenly pulled out a long kitchen knife, and while Hank, being stronger and quicker than Sean, dodged his attack and subdued him, I dialed 911.

When the Bronx police showed up, they took a brief statement from both Hank and Sean and then told them to go their separate ways. I told the police that I had called them and I was in fact a witness to the entire incident, but they were not impressed nor did they see any sense of urgency. They told me that, since they hadn't seen who originally possessed the knife, they wouldn't press any criminal charges against Sean, and strongly suggested that everyone go on their merry way, although, of course, if we wanted to, we could file separate complaints according to what our version was. Other than that, we all had to move along.

After that violent display, I knew that I was not safe at Hank's anymore. The fact that Sean tried to lure me out of the house vowing remorse for his violent behavior, only to lure me outside so that he could kill me was terrifying. Overwhelmed with a sense of hopelessness, I realized that everything that I did to protect myself would count another check mark against me in Sean's twisted sense of righteousness.

I called a cab and returned home to collect Marie and pack, hoping that for the next few hours, at least, Sean would be too preoccupied with his father's funeral, which was to take place that afternoon, to continue to pursue me, only to find my answering machine filled with incoming messages. Four in a row were Sean's menacing voice screaming repeated threats against me.

In his first message Sean said, "Guess what. I know everything about you, Sweetheart. Take my word for it—Hanks' not going to stop me this time. You can go fuck yourself in life because even though I might have a little dick, you're the fuckin' biggest whore I ever fucking met in my life!" Sheer terror shot through my body as I continued to listen to his messages. In the second one he said, "I hope you have the Darien police there because, you're going to be in trouble too—you hear me? You got it? So you might as well forget about work for three or four days. "His threats were real and direct but his words were jumbled and mixed up. His voice was so primal and salvage that its rawness crept into my bones. His third message was more evidence of his distorted mind. "You made the wrong move!" he shouted. . . . "I'm going in the witness protection program to protect myself from my brother who just beat my face in. You're a no good fuckin slut. That's all you've ever been in your whole fuckin' life . . . You can go fuck yourself and you can tell your buddy with the gun I'm coming after him, too!" That message and the one that followed were much the same.

I followed his advice and immediately called the Darien police department. Officer Percy Packs was on duty that evening. He came to my house to investigate my phone complaint. I was hysterical as I played the messages for Officer Packs who was clearly taken aback. This was the same officer who had once told me that I should shoot Sean, drag him into the house, and that the police would come clean up the mess. Now, he suggested that I come up with a plan to get Sean over from New York into Connecticut, explaining that Sean being in the Bronx obstructed Connecticut authorities from arresting him since New York was out of their jurisdiction. I suggested that I have a few guys who were aikido experts go to the city and bring Sean back to Connecticut. His response was that anyone who did that could face kidnapping charges for forcing him over the New York State line. I was out of ideas to trick Sean to come over the state-line willingly.

When Marie called from her girlfriend's house, I explained what had happened and that the police were with me now, but that she should not come home yet, that we were devising a plan to lure Sean into Connecticut jurisdiction.

Talking to my daughter gave me an idea. I would call Sean and tell him that Marie had been taken to the hospital because of an asthma attack and that she was asking for him. And so, with Office Packs standing beside me, I called Sean and told him that Marie was really ill, suggesting that he take the train. And when he agreed, Officer Packs informed the Stamford Police of his estimated arrival so that they could arrest him.

And so it happened that, when Sean stepped onto the platform, a swat team of armed police officers took him into custody, handcuffing him and placing him in the squad car. As ironic as it was, he was arrested in the same building that he had previously assaulted me.

TWELVE

Only Escape-Death of Abuser

GIVEN MY PREVIOUS EXPERIENCE WITH the Darien police's procedure over the Thanksgiving Eve's arrest and release, I didn't have much faith in their holding Sean long term either. I was still shaken and unconvinced that Sean would remain in police custody, certainly not calm enough to stay at my house alone, I again pack up some necessities and drove off to Hank's house for the remainder of that evening. I figured that the South Bronx was quite a distance for Sean to travel if, by chance, he was released. I had better odds of survival by staying at his brother's house, than being at my home which was located, in a quiet and secluded neighborhood.

Before I left the house, I called both the Darien and Stamford police stations because I had to know that Sean was, in fact, still in custody and was assured that I was on alert status and that, if Sean were released from jail, they would notify me personally. The Fairfield County Jail was to notify the Stamford police, and in turn, they would alert the Darien police, who would call me. In theory, it seems like a great protective precaution. However, it was not even close to what actually took place.

I kept swallowing pills to enable me to control the intense tremors that jolted through my body, my nerves so on edge that they were like frayed electrical wires as I kept replaying the messages that Sean had left for me on my answering machine. "I know everything about you sweetheart . . . You better get the Darien police after me . . ." I felt absolutely trapped, with no way out. Sean was clearly determined to kill me. The fact that I had him arrested again meant that he was going to count that as another strike against me. It was, for him, another nail in my coffin.

I drove over to Hank's house all the while knowing that this was only a temporary shelter for me, taking my gun along, and once there I continued to pop nerve pills, washing them down with straight vodka. At one point that evening I remember falling down his staircase and landing on the hardwood floor at the base of the steps, but the remainder of that night was a complete void for me until, that evening before Christmas Eve and a busy time at the salon, I had to drive to work the next morning, only to arrive there so groggy and disheveled that I had to explain to my boss, Katie, that, although Sean was presently in jail, I was convinced that he would get out and kill me. In a letter Katie wrote, "About nine in the morning, she walked in the front door of the Salon . . . and when I looked up I couldn't believe what I saw. She was staggering, her eyes looked almost shut and she was shaking uncontrollably. I stood up and said, 'What happened to you!' I had never seen anyone look so bad or so scared before. She looked like someone I didn't even know!"

In the short time I was there, a phone call came for me from the hospital in Darien telling me that Marie had been actually been taken there by ambulance for an asthma attack. At that, I began to cry uncontrollably. I was in such bad shape that I had to be driven to the hospital by a coworker, named Vickie.

When we arrived, Marie was in the emergency unit, already receiving medical help. When I went to her and held her hand, a woman dressed in a pant suit introduced herself as a social worker and asked me to step into the hallway with her. First she wanted to know if I had been drinking, and when I told her no, explained to me that Marie had informed her that her father was abusive and that he had recently been arrested for assaulting me. And when I confirmed that her information was correct, she told me that Marie would not be able to return home until an investigator from the Division of Family Services made an inspection and was able to report that Marie would be safe there. She took the name and phone number of Marie's friend and suggested that she remain at her house until an investigation took place and a determination was made. I was granted permission to take Marie home and pick up clothes for her before she had to leave to stay at her friends. A few hours later, Marie was released from the emergency ward into my care.

By the time Vickie, Marie and I got into the car and headed home, I was beside myself. Despite everything that was happening, now my own child would be unable to be with me. One by one, Sean had slowly taken everything away from me, and. I fell into a dark cavern filled with despair, weakened by hopelessness. My will to fight had vanished.

As I arrived home on Christmas Eve, my stepfather pulled up at the same time, and I ran to him, weeping and explaining that not only was Sean going to kill me, but Marie had to leave the house because of him. I asked him to take care of Marie if anything bad happened to me. And after promising me that he would, he advised me to get some sleep and drove home, leaving Vicki to stay with me awhile.

I so desperately wanted to sleep and never wake up, to never again have to worry about Sean coming after me that I was totally overwhelmed. And so I decided to take the whole bottle of Sean's Librium medication, only to wake to find my daughter and my mother shaking me. Marie was screaming, "What did you do? What did you take? Wake up, please wake up!" I remember getting up feeling like my head weighed a ton. Staggering into the bathroom, I splashed cold water on my face and forced myself to vomit, after which I begged both my mother and daughter not to report what had happened since a suicide attempt would only complicate the problem.

I didn't awaken until the phone rang late Christmas day. Forcing my way to consciousness, I picked up the receiver to find that it was my mother calling to check on me. After I convinced her that I was fine, Marie arrived to open her presents. I don't remember much of that day other than drinking vodka and swallowing nerve pills in order to throw my body into a catatonic state of stillness. That evening, alone and desperate to ease my pain, I thought about shooting myself in the head. I sat on my bed facing the front windows and held the gun to my right temple, pressing the cold metal barrel firmly against my skin. I held it there for what seemed like forever, and then I lowered my arm. I didn't even have enough guts to shoot myself. I was disgusted with my lack of courage. Out of pure frustration, I quickly fired two shots into the wall in front of me, and then walked downstairs to the kitchen to take more Xanax in order to knock myself into a sound sleep.

Vickie called the next morning to tell me that she was going to stop over to see me. I had been up on and off all day, hysterically trying to figure out how I was going to move away to safety. Vickie later wrote, "The day after Christmas I went to visit Margo at about three in the afternoon and found her chain smoking and drinking vodka, completely out of control because of her fear that Sean was going to kill her. There is no question in my mind that she was confident that he would do that."

After a few futile calls to the police in both counties to ask for protection, Vicky later wrote, "I remember Margo telling the Darien police that she needed to know whether Sean Donnelly had been bailed out because, if he had, he was going to kill her. I personally spoke to a Darien police officer that night and asked the officer if there was some way to get protection but he was unresponsive, although we did learn that Sean's bail had been reduced to ten percent. In desperation, we tried to contract a private detective, but due to the holidays, could find no one in their office. I was with Margo for about five hours on that Sunday night until about eight, and she remained convinced that Sean was going to come and kill her."

By now I was convinced that Sean would call his sister Colleen and manipulate her into bailing him out, certain that she might give in in the hopes that he would share his father's life insurance benefits. I even imagined the possibility of Sean calling one of his hoodlum friends from the city, and offering to pay them a nice sum of money to post bail for him. The bottom line was that I feared that Sean would be out of jail and on a direct route to end my life. And sure enough, one of my calls to the Darien police elicited the fact that, although I had not been notified, he had, indeed, been released on bail.

When Vickie had to go to her friend's for the night, I really fell into hysterics at the thought of being left alone, but when I told Marie that I was losing my grip, she said that she had explained everything to her friend Mindy and that she had volunteered to keep a watch over me and try to keep me calm until the next day. Vickie left my house as Mindy knocked on the door, and the phone rang with a collect call from the Fairfield County Correctional Facility. My first reaction was relief that Sean was still there and so I accepted the charges, determined to seem unafraid.

It came as no real surprise when he went into a soulful plea for my forgiveness for his transgressions toward me, and then began the "Poor Sean" phase, going on and on about how his father's death had pushed him over the edge. And then, without skipping a beat, he vowed to never hurt me again if I just came and got him out of there. Sean's response did not amaze me, but was all too familiar a tune for me to fall for it again. It was Sean's pattern of manipulation to get what he wanted out of me, just as a few days previous at his brother's house when he vowed not hurt me if I came out and meet with him when, all the while, he had had a large kitchen knife under his coat ready to stab me to death. I knew Sean's shallow promises stood for bait to get what he needed from me, but let him talk on and on for over ten minutes before I told him I would have to think about it because I didn't want him to call his sister under any circumstances. I knew that she would fall for his lies probably feel sorry for him and go get him out of jail. I needed to know that he was behind bars.

Mindy was a tower of strength and it was she, in the end, who came up with a solution, one which, had I been in my right mind, I would have rejected. As a former member of a City gang, she knew, she said, ways of taking care of Sean forever, particularly since it was clear that he would not stop until he had killed me. "It's simple self-defense," she said before outlining a plan in which, if I would provide the bail, she would see that Sean never endangered anyone again.

In the end, I ran upstairs and took one thousand dollars out of my safety box, and with the gun in my coat pocket, Mindy and I set off to the Darien police station to post bail for Sean's release. It was a short drive to the police station. Dizzy and groggy from the nerve pills and vodka mixture, I placed the handgun in the side pocket of the driver's seat when Mindy pulled into the police parking lot. Mindy left me in the locked car where, after climbing in the back, I promptly passed out. When she came back to the car, the doors were locked and afraid that I was unconscious, she was forced to face the fact that I might have died from an overdose.

It took Mindy over forty-five minutes to break into my car, and just when she finally managed it, I saw Sean, now out on the bail I had provided Mindy, stepping off of a Fairfield County transport bus. Every nerve in my body screamed with terror, and desperate to escape, I crawled into the trunk, unseen by him, although I heard his voice and Mindy's and finally we were back on the road, the rocking of the car, combined with the remains of vodka in my system, lulling me to sleep.

The next thing I remember was the trunk opening and Mindy standing over me, shaking my shoulder and saying, "It's over, I did it. I shot him. He didn't see it coming." I jumped up in disbelief and saw that we were in a long deserted wooded driveway. Running to the passenger side of the car, I saw Sean, his head slumped on his chest but because there wasn't a speck of blood in view, I suspected that this was a set-up, my inner voice telling me that this must be an ambush, that Sean and Mindy had somehow planned to get me out there into the woods, and that he was finally going to get me. But when I saw, or thought I saw, him move, I screamed that he was still alive. At that moment a shot rang out and I saw blood trickling from his nose and mouth.

"It all over," I heard Mindy say, and suddenly she was hugging me. "He can't get you anymore. It's over! You're safe now!" Although I was in shock, my first impulse was to tell Mindy that we had to put Sean into the trunk of the car because there was no way that we could drive through the streets with a body in the front seat. Mindy grabbed his arms and I took his legs and, struggling, put him in the trunk and covered the body with the blanket. Mindy talked non-stop as we drove back into Darien, explaining that, when he had recognized my car, she had told him that I had given it to her so that she could pick him up, and had added that she knew a place where he could get drugs.

Pulling up in front of my house was somewhat of a relief. The moment we were inside, I gave Mindy the phone to make a call to her buddy Jake who sold her drugs from time to time, and who she felt confident would help us. But when she told him that we had just shot a guy and that she needed his help, Jake apparently thought that she was high and possibly hallucinating. And when she handed the phone to me and I told this complete stranger that Mindy has just shot my abusive boyfriend, and that we needed him to lend us a car, he hung up on me thinking that I was playing a prank on him. Mindy called Jake again but he refused to talk to her about it which left us still without a car to transport Sean's body to a woodsy area. Finally, I suggested that we move Sean into the house, just as the Darien police officer Percy Packs had told me to do months before. However, Mindy told me it was already too late for that, because Sean had been dead for too long a period of time.

I racked my brain trying to think of someone that I could call for help until I thought of Ishmal, and sure enough, when I called him and said that I was in trouble and needed his help, he said that he could be right over, and within what seemed like minutes he was there. When he saw the gun on the coffee table, he looked seriously concerned. He looked at Mindy seated across the living room and then whispered in my ear, "Is she cool to talk in front of?" I answered him by saying, "Yes, of course she is. She was the one who shot Sean." After that, I told him the entire story.

When Ishmal wanted to know what I had planned on doing, I again stated that I wanted to bring Sean's body into my house and then call the police, but he agreed with Mindy that too much time had passed for me to claim that Sean had just been shot, and suggested that we move the body into the trunk of his car which we subsequently did, unseen by neighbors since dawn was just breaking. And then, with my nerves as raw as live wires, we drove to the wooded area near the Wetlands where we planned to dispose of Sean's body, a process that was more difficult than we had foreseen. Although Mindy was taller and heavier than I, Sean was heavier still, particularly now that rigor mortis had set in. But once we accomplished it and Mindy had thrown the gun into the brush we jumped in the car and prepared to take off.

Only then did the full impact of what had happened strike me. I was so shaken up that I floored the gas petal and caused the car's tires to spin in the sandy earth below it. I kept stepping on the gas until the tires dug deeper into the earth's natural gravel. Finally, the car was sunken into the dirt road so deeply that we had to dig the tires out with sticks to give us traction. Once the car started, we only stopped long enough to get rid of the blanket in which Sean's body had been wrapped, throwing it into a trashcan. After that I don't believe that I stopped again, not even for red lights, until we were home again.

Mindy went upstairs and took a shower while I ran all around my house like a loose cannon, trying to figure out what I was going to do about my car which, fortunately, was spattered with very little blood that was easily removed by cutting out bits of fabric which covered the seat in which Sean had been sitting. And then, even though it was, I suppose, illogical, I went to a body shop and paid seven hundred dollars to have the window that Mindy had broken in her attempt to get into the car replaced.

Looking back, I guess that I thought that if I could remove all the evidence of the crime, it might just as well not have happened. And in the process of all this frantic activity, I ran into John whom I had met years ago when he had repossessed my car after Scott had forgotten to make payments on it, and then helped me get it out of hock.

John was a very rough looking individual, covered with tattoos, one in particular being a snake wrapped around his neck and looking as though it were about to hiss. When he asked how I liked the car, I told him that it was okay, and when he looked inside and saw the seat covers, I told him that kids had vandalized it and rip up the seats and had broken my windshield. And when I said that I wanted to get rid of it, he offered to burn it for six hundred dollars, to which I eagerly agreed, I welcomed his suggestion that we meet for dinner that night and he would make my car disappear.

A message from Colleen was waiting for me when I got home. She was concerned about Sean's release, having called the Fairfield County jail and been told that someone had bailed Sean out. The hair on my neck rose at the thought of speaking with Colleen, but I knew that I had to return her call. When she answered the phone and immediately asked me if I had heard or seen Sean, I lied and told her no. She said that the jail facility had informed her that a female named Mindy Molee had bailed him out late the night before, but I professed to know nothing about that, although I agreed to call her if I heard from Sean. When I hung up the phone, I had to hold myself up by hanging onto the unit attached to the kitchen wall.

Mindy had apparently left, so after jumping in the shower, I went into my bedroom and stretched across my bed. My intention was to close my eyes for just a few moments, but totally exhausted, I fell into a deep sleep for hours. When I finally awoke, my bedroom was completely black, with the exception of, the glimmer of the outside street light. For a brief moment, I had imagined that the entire late night and early morning events were just a bad dream. And when I slowly realized that it was not a dream but a terrible reality, I thought about going to the police and telling them about what had happened. I quickly shook off the idea and focused on what I had to do next, only then remembering that I had agreed to meet John for dinner in less than a half an hour. Quickly pulling myself together, I drove away from my house. It was December 27, 1993, the last day that I would ever see my Darien, Connecticut home again.

THIRTEEN

Criminal Arrest

DINNER WITH JOHN PROVIDED ME with two reassurances. I was able to give him the second and last set of car keys, and without asking questions, he told me not to worry about the car, because he would make sure it was unrecognizable. He told me how he intended to obliterate the car by setting it ablaze. Although I never revealed the reason for wanting my car destroyed, I told him that it was important to douse the trunk completely because there was some blood there and allowed him to assume the rest; I presume he did, because he told me to report the car missing forty-five minutes after he left the restaurant.

While I waited, I dialed my mother's phone number and impatiently listened to each ring. And when her voice came over the line, as soothing as a warm soft blanket, on a cold winter's day, I felt an instantaneous calm wash over me. After letting her know that I was safe, and reassuring her that I was out of harm's way, I began to cry, explaining that I had done something terrible and that I was in big trouble, whereupon she suddenly interrupted me in mid-sentence, saying, "Margo, don't you tell me anything you might have done. The only thing that matters is that you are okay." I didn't understand why she abruptly stopped me from telling her what had happened, but later I came to realize that she might have been legally obligated to testify against me. I ask her to please take care of my daughter in the event that I was unable to even though there was no question that she would not rise to the challenge. I didn't have to ask her to take Marie. I just needed to verbalize it so that I could ease my mind. I told my mother that I loved her and I hung up the phone.

I forced myself to think of the traumatic events that had occurred in the last twenty-four hours in the hope that I would seem convincingly distraught when reporting my car missing to the police. But when I told them my name, the officer announced that there was an all-points bulletin out for my arrest for murder.

After escorting me outside, the police officer pointed his weapon at me, and demanded that I raise my hands slowly over my head, patting me down to see if I was armed before handcuffing me so tightly that I winced. The other officer recited my Miranda rights and then guided me into the back seat of the car where I sank down feeling both shocked and relieved. Although I was astounded by the rapid occurrences taking place, I was relieved that I would not have to run anymore.

I was driven to the Darien police station for questioning where I was placed, still handcuffed, in a small holding cell for so long that I curled up on a hard wooden bench and fell asleep. When the hallway light streaking across my face brought me to a semi-conscious state, I was not quite sure where I was until the handcuffs cutting into my wrists reminded me of what had happened. A Detective Wyatt appeared to take me into an interrogation room, and he explained how he was going to help me.

I welcomed his assistance. I had never been arrested before in my life and was not familiar with the legal system or how it worked. I was brought up to believe that authorities were to be trusted, and taught to respect police officers who were there to protect and serve with integrity and honesty. Detective Wyatt reminded me that he had been there when I had originally come, hysterical, into his police station. He relayed his understanding of how I could have been driven to commit murder, squeezing my hand gently in an attempt to make me aware of his empathy. It never dawned on me to ask to speak with an attorney, even though I must have been read my Miranda rights.

When he left, I was joined by a man who said that he had spoken with Detective Wyatt and that, in his opinion, the legal system had failed me, leaving me feeling as though he had spoken with a family member. The mood of the room changed abruptly when Detective Wyatt appeared to announce that he did not believe that my neighbor Mindy had shot Sean, and that he needed to hear the truth, in order to help me. I kept saying that I was telling him exactly what had happened, to which he claimed, made no sense at all. A black officer who joined him seemed to find my explanation equally absurd.

After hours of interrogation on limited sleep and under an influence that equaled extreme duress, I was ready to give them whatever they requested, particularly since I so desperately needed to speak to my daughter and my mother, something that they assured me would happen when I became more cooperative which meant, as I came to understand, when I told them what they wanted to hear. Fighting them to explain the truth seemed like a useless battle, particularly since I felt guilty about the circumstances that had led to Sean's death. And so I decided to appease them with the answers they believed to be true. It was then that I took on the responsibility for Sean's death, including the actual shooting, allowing whatever Detective Wyatt surmised to be put on record.

Feeling defeated and exhausted, I listened to Detective Wyatt's questions and then confirmed the answers he fed me. Whenever I gave him an answer that he was not happy with, he would interject what he thought happened. I would then agree and repeat his suggestion. It was over an hour of the fill-in-the-blanks game. Detective Wyatt had Sean being shot at a convenience store in Darien, Connecticut. He had me getting out of the trunk, in the parking lot in order to shoot Sean right there in a well-lit parking lot, although that didn't make any sense

The detective's presumption seemed absurd to me, but it was what he envisioned. He was convinced that I had shot Sean in that exact location and I could not convince him otherwise. And so it was that I went along with this ridiculous idea of his "logical" conclusion. When he was pretty certain that I had the entire spoon-fed information perfected, he brought in his partner and started the process all over again, the only difference being that, this time, he used an audio tape recording, for proof of my so-called labeled confession of the crime. It was good cop, bad cop, worst cop, lying cop with no holds bar in order to get what they needed to get. It was a true awaking for me.

There was no question of my going home. There were no hugs from my mother or my daughter. Instead I was placed back into the holding cell, until they transported me to the County Prosecutor's Office where I had samples of my hair plucked, my saliva swabbed and my body checked for any specific markings.

Hours later, I was able to make a two minute telephone call to my mother. The moment I had awaited had finally arrived. After over eight hours of psychological bombardment, I received the okay and dialed my mother's number. The moment I heard her voice, my words stumbled over one another as I tried to condense all that had happened to me into a two minute call. The long and short of it was that I was at the prosecutor's office, located in Bridgeport. I left out the fact that I was in need of an attorney. My mother told me to hold on and try to remain calm. She would, she said, find a lawyer for me. When I hung up the phone, I felt like I was out in the middle of the ocean without a lifeline.

When Mindy was escorted into the room minutes later, I saw, to my horror and amazement that she was wearing Sean's sweat pants, but when I pointed that out, she said, "Why not? He doesn't need them anymore." That was all I needed to be certain that this woman, who I had thought was a friend, was a sociopath.

After being transferred to the Fairfield County Jail for processing, both Mindy and I were charged and booked on one count indictment of first-degree murder. I was later served with twelve other indictment counts of various crimes that were related to that single incident.

The next stop was the County Correctional Facility where we were fingerprinted, photographed, showered, deloused and given an orange jump suit before receiving a mattress, sheet and a torn black blanket and locked in what I learned were called holding cells. At no time was Mindy given an opportunity to speak to me, no doubt because they did not want us to coordinate our stories. After being processed, I was transferred down a narrow hallway leading to the officer's central station, a circular command center, which was encapsulated in glass facing three different units, two small women's units called B and C blocks and a larger one called A block which housed the general population of women. The two smaller units for inmates that were medically disabled, and work released was called C block. Lastly the mentally incompetent and disciplinary problems resided in what was called B Block.

The large glass paneled doors were controlled by an automatic remote system, operated by the officers in the central station and consisted of twenty rooms, each with two bunk beds, a stainless steel sink, a toilet, and a small metal desk with a built-in seat which was bolted to the wall. Each room was approximately ten feet long by seven feet wide. The room the doors of solid metal with a porthole window situated so high that I had to jump up to peek out. The main day room had steel benches and televisions, which were mounted to the ceiling. The jail was so over-populated that women were sleeping on the day room floor. They also assigned three women to each room, one in each bed, and one mattress on the floor beside the toilet which was the space allotted me until, folding my "bed" in half, I pushed it against the door, as far as I possibly could, although not far enough to keep me from hearing the women in the general population yelling at me through the room door.

I heard them saying, "Hey look at her," and "She's so tiny, and she looks all bruised up. Hey, girl! Come to the window! Don't be afraid. You don't look like you killed nobody!" I looked up at the window and saw several faces peering down at me. I could feel the door banging and vibrating, as the women fought one another to sneak a peek at me. Quickly placing the scratchy, tattered blanket over my head, I began to shake and cry hysterically. Completely traumatized by what had happened, I wanted to use the phone to call my mother. I kept praying that the door wouldn't open under any circumstances as I had been told that I would be locked in my room for a total of seven days until I was given medical clearance. I was so relieved that I would be separated from that savage crowd. As far as I was concerned, they could have locked me in that room for my entire time there. I didn't want anything to do with those spectators that gawked through the circular window. I stayed under the blanket and cried until the women stopped hanging on the door.

I welcomed the sight of the correctional officer. My door clicked open and in the doorway stood a black woman dressed in a chocolate brown uniform whose silver badge read, "Ms. Andrews". She had gentle eyes but a firm voice and told me that I could come out to use the phone and to take a shower. I told her I was afraid to be out there with those women, who were looking through my window. She let me know that it was after lock-in so all the other detainees were locked in their rooms. I slowly emerged from the cell with my towel in hand.

After that, I used the phone to call my mother. The moment she accepted the collect call, hot tears rolled down my cheeks. "Please help me, Mother," I cried. "It's not safe in this place. The people are staring at me through the window in my room. Where is Marie? Tell her I'm sorry and that I love her! Please help me."

My mother was working on finding a lawyer but I could hear the desperation in her voice. She wanted to keep me strong and focused, while her heart ached from her inability to fix my situation. I was hurting and she felt my pain vicariously.

I remained awake all night. All I wanted to do was watch the sunrise, because then I would again be granted the privilege of calling home. The next morning came and although I was told several times that I would be able to call, somehow that never happened even though I cried for hours on end. Every time the officer came around I begged her to let me out to use the phone but apparently it was not convenient for her to unlock my door, escort me to the phone area, and then lock me back in the cell.

Hours later, the next shift of officers came on duty, and by then I was so frantic that I wanted to die. I was trying to hook my blanket, twisted into a noose, up to the cell's light fixture, when my cellmates screamed for the other women to call the correctional officer. The next thing I knew the door clicked and two officers took me into a side room that they used for attorney visits where Officer Mason informed me that I was being transferred to the mental unit. She told me to be strong, and to pray to God for strength.

After that, she took me into the smaller unit and showed me to a cell where she introduced me to a black woman named Marita and asked her to watch over me. When Marita grumbled about the door being locked for seven days, the officer agreed to allow it to remain unlocked, but made it clear that I had to stay inside the room because of medical segregation.

Marita was living in that unit because of a fight with one of the other inmates. She was kind enough to me, and because I cried so much, called me "Boo-Boo". Despite her grim exterior, she was kind and empathetic and she helped to make me feel so safe that I was convinced that my God had placed me in her cell to give me some peace.

Meanwhile, I resided with the mentally incompetent and disciplinary problematic detainee in a truly predatory arena. The televisions suspended from the ceiling broadcasted different local news channels, the announcer's voices echoing throughout the steel coated cellblock. The women shushed the others as the incoming announcements beamed across the airwaves.

In my case, there was a media feeding frenzy. As they received it, the local and national news filtered bits and pieces of obtained information. My crime was initially labeled the "Thelma and Louise" killing. This identification stuck with Mindy and me for the duration, although the only similarity was that Mindy shot Sean for me, just as Louise shot the rapist for Thelma. Other than that, everything else was far off the mark. By the time the media became privy to the real circumstances surrounding the crime, along with the history of abuse, many of the newscasters showed sympathy toward me, although, the Thelma and Louise title never quite disappeared.

The unit's televisions blasted the updated versions of the Thelma and Louise killing as all of my cellmates attentively focused on each and every word spoken. They stood in the day room with their eyes glued to the talking black boxes dangling from the ceiling.

The group's live wire, Sharonda was all of five feet tall. She had been placed in this unit because she had attacked a woman in the general population unit. Having been arrested several times prior to this current stint, she had a record of repeated drug and armed robbery related offenses. This time around she was in jail for the long haul. The first time I saw her, she was sitting on the top of the metal table in the day room, facing the automatic doors. Looking straight at me coming through the glass doors, she said, "Welcome to the Broken Cookie Box. We're all broken cookies here in this housing unit. Girl, tell them you crazy, Tell 'em you want to go to the Hartford State Mental Hospital for evaluation. You were insane when you killed him. That's what you do. You say you lost your mind. Be smart, girl, and say you crazy!"

I was called out of my room several times for visits from different licensed attorneys. I had so many lawyers coming to the jail requesting to speak with me that I felt as though my cell had a revolving door attached to the hinges. I wasn't sure what to say to them so I told them my parents had hired representation for me.

Again, my presence was requested in the attorney visiting area. I walked out through the unit's glass doors. I saw a familiar friendly face staring at me, from across the hallway. Seated at a table, next to the glass window, was my former client Sharon Ravitz. It was refreshing to cast my eyes on someone familiar. Sharon had just graduated from the local university in Connecticut. She had taken the bar exam only months earlier and, since my parents did not yet have an attorney of record, she wanted to come see me and offer her assistance. Sharon spoke with her college professor who happened to be well versed in Battered Women's Syndrome and suggested that she take on my case, offering to team up with her to provide both guidance and assistance.

But, attorney or not, there were indignities to follow. When a female officer escorted me to my unit, I was instructed to raise my hands and spread my legs so that I could be patted down, in search of possible contraband. Ironically, I returned in time for lunch to be served. There was a built-in latch door carved into the glass paneled wall. A correctional officer used a large key to open the small passageway. She then yelled, "Chows up", and an inmate served each tray through the latch door. The trays, which were bulky plastic colored gold or brown with preformed divisions for separation of different foods, were stacked up on the concrete floor outside the unit's glass doors. A side of applesauce and a juice accompanied bologna sandwiches on white bread. The smell of sour mop mixed with packaged lunchmeat permeated the room. The whole process was enough to take away any appetite I had acquired.

My high hopes in regard to representation were dashed that day when my parents decided not to accept Sharon's offer and contacted a New York firm to represent me on the basis of a recommendation by one of Mel's friends who had, coincidentally, won a defense of a young woman, now serving as their secretary.

I spent hours with them explaining every detail of the crime and found them very professional, empathic and confident. I was told not to speak with anyone about my case but they wanted me to begin writing my entire history with Sean. This would give them a more detailed documentation for use in building my defense. They had to arrange to take photographs of the bruising on different parts of my body after some of his attacks, and informed me that I would have to appear at an arraignment hearing at the week's end, to briefly review the legal proceedings that would occur. I attempted to absorb all of the information, but was so overcome with emotion that one of then, a man named Jay promised to return the next day.

I finished the evening off by furiously writing down everything I could remember about my life with Sean, jogging my memory so that I could go back to the age of thirteen. I wrote until the lights were turned off and I continued writing by using the outside light shining in from the narrow window until, at about one in the morning, I was abruptly informed that I was being put in another cell where a sympathetic woman named Maryann was waiting to welcome me and listen to my story. It never occurred to me until later that she was a snitch, and that the prosecution had collaborated with the state to offer her a deal in which her sentence would be reduced if she were willing to swear that I confessed to her that I, not Mindy, was guilty of murder.

But at the time, I knew nothing of this. As the sun rose, peeking through the window, the cell door clicked open and Officer Mason told me to follow her with my belongings, taking me back to Block B while explaining that my middle-of-the-night move was not on the schedule.

Later that day, Sharon Ravitz arrived at the lawyer's visiting hall. I was so glad to see her again that I told her that my parents had hired a few attorneys from a law firm in New York. She seemed relieved that I had an attorney of record, saying that it took the pressure off her. We talked for a short while before my attorney, Jay Jaron, arrived. Sharon offered to go down to the private room and help videotape me and take photos of my body. Since she was a woman, it made it an easier task to be naked to film all of the bruises. Still it was extremely humiliating and uncomfortable to stand in the center of a room, stripped down in front of a former client, a correctional officer and a male lawyer. Officer Mason held up a sheet in front of me, so that my naked body was not in plain view of my newly hired male attorney. I was thrilled to quickly jump back into my strange orange jumpsuit.

That was the last time I was able to visit with Sharon Ravitz because my attorneys filed a form at the jail that stopped all lawyers from visiting me without the direct consent of their law firm. This request was for my protection, because the prosecutor's office had sent an attorney up to question me. He was fishing around, questioning whether or not I had an attorney of record. A multitude of lawyers scurried up to meet me. All the legal hopefuls were nipping at the heels of the media. The media tumult was truly a circus act. Attorneys were definitely interested in appearing on the nightly news. Local news channels that spotlighted my case served as a motivational thrust for many licensed professionals that were thirsty for attention.

The newsworthiness of my case made way for a host of unwanted letters and request for interviews. Several television show hosts had sent me Federal Express letters requesting my appearance on their talk shows. Willard Thomas, who was the host for *New York Today,* made several attempts for an exclusive. Most of the broadcast personalities contacted my attorneys for permission to schedule a statement about my case, from me, my family or my attorneys themselves. Each one of the local channels and daily newspapers were persistent in pursing my story.

As more information came across to each of these news stations, they made public a daily diet of retractions and updates regarding the events leading up to Sean's death. As the evidence of abuse became better known the news media scrambled for more details. Their information came from a mixture of personal interviews and shared police reports. They were all out and about, feeding from any source they could obtain. All the news stations were trying to be the first one to get an exclusive interview. The media sent reporters out to the salon I had worked at and interviewed many of my former coworkers, employers and my friends. They were also able to obtain names of my former boyfriends, friends and family members. And they swarmed outside of my parent's home in an attempt to interview anyone. They found the name of my former gym and showed up there trying to get a statement from anyone who was remotely familiar with me, leaving no stone unturned in their search for anyone who was willing to give them a few words regarding my past. My attorneys gave them an interview on the basis that they had to set the record straight, given the amount of the misinformation the new media had gathered. Local news reporters were without shame in cultivating a story. They chased Sean's family for comments as well as my own family. His brother Hank made a statement, to the local New York news, saying that his brother Sean was a very sick individual. Hank went on to say that the entire situation was unfortunate but inevitable and went on to explain that he and his family had tried to get Sean help for his addictions. He stated that Sean and my relationship had always been destined to end in tragedy.

As the media gathered more factual history about my story, it was venturing further away from the original label of the "Thelma and Louise" killing. At the immediate inception of my crime, the media was quick to surmise a diabolic scenario, but as more information materialized, they focused more on the true underlying reasoning, for such a drastic act to have taken place. The abuse I suffered at the hands of Sean then became the focus of their attention with the result that my desperation became an important part of the story.

FOURTEEN

Court Arraignment

ARRAIGNMENT FOR THE CRIMINAL CHARGES of first-degree murder, coupled with hindering prosecution made for a full courtroom of people. Spectators, witnesses, opposing party and media reporters packed every square inch of the Fairfield County Courthouse.

A female correctional officer escorted me down the hallway. As I walked, my sanitary pad fell into the leg of my cuffed jumpsuit, leaving me no option but to attempt to stick a pad to my narrow thong type underwear. I pleaded with the correctional officer to please take me back to my unit because of my personal problem. She understood and was nice enough to find someone to give me a tampon. That was just the beginning to a total humiliating day.

My hands were cuffed with metal bracelets attached to a thick leather belt, which was anchored around my waist. My legs were then shackled in metal anklets and tied to one another by a four inch linked chain. My boots, which had been taken away when I was arrested were now replaced by a pair of size eleven black rubber flip-flops which I had to struggle to keep on.

As I entered the crowded courtroom, all I heard was the clicking and snapping of cameras. Telescopic lens were pointed at me as if they were missiles in a military mission. I was guided to a large dark wooden table where my newly appointed legal representatives were seated. Turning around, I saw my daughter and my mother seated behind me and a lump rose in my throat.

The judge, an aged man with white hair, dressed in the standard black robe turned out to be someone who was accustomed to filtering out evidence to meet his requirements, and sifted out any mitigating factors surrounding my experience. Consequently, he set the sum of two hundred thousand dollar cash bail the minute that I pleaded not guilty even though my attorney, Mr. Mushin, argued that this crime had not been committed in cold blood. He revisited the history of abuse that had driven me to desperation and offered the mitigating facts of my criminal free record, law-abiding lifestyle, along with the fact that I was a single mother, hard worker, and homeowner. Numerous individuals offered their support with strong ties to the community before asking that my bail be reduced to a reasonable amount. Unfortunately, his words fell upon deaf ears.

A short while later, my attorneys met with me upstairs. In an effort to calm me down and show their game face for the big fight ahead, they did everything in their power to hide their disappointment, and made plans to forge ahead with Plan B. This was a definite deviation from concentrating on building my defense. However, it was necessary to prepare such a motion to show the opposition our stand on reasonable justice. They had called in the firm's research professionals to gather up legal cases, in support of their argument on the motion for bail reduction, ready to fight the system for the sheer injustice. I was not so ready to put up such a fight. I was broken down mentally and physically distraught, weakened to the point of total surrender. This was yet just the beginning of a long arduous legal battle during which I was inducted into the legal arena without any knowledge of what awaited me. At that point in time, I only had my idea of what was fair and just. I soon was taught, through direct experience, that the word fair had no correlation to the justice system.

I was actually relieved to enter the women's unit, where I could be locked in my small cell. I sat on my bed and cried for all of the wrong choices I had made, for the individuals I had hurt and for the current circumstance I found myself in.

I called home just to hear my daughter's voice. She was expecting to have me back with her and it broke my heart to hear the disappointment in her voice which cracked as each word came over the telephone line. I told her to hang on and be strong and that I will be home with her soon. Desperate to have her mom back, she was becoming increasingly impatient with the wait. She handed the receiver to my mother whose hopeful words gave me the strength to continue the fight.

Shortly after our phone conversation, my mother suffered a massive stroke. She was rushed to the local hospital intensive care unit and survived the unexpected blood clot with only a slight paralysis on her right side. The aftermath resulted in her having to drag her right leg, and the immobility of her right arm and hand, and one side of her face to droop. Lastly her speech was dramatically slurred. I blamed myself for her condition. I knew that the stress of my situation indeed played a role in her failing health. As she forced herself to gather enough strength to push forward, I prayed every day for God not to take my mother away from us. I prayed for forgiveness and found myself bargaining with god for the opportunity to make up for my mistakes.

My mother's condition made me want to give up. I didn't want to drag her through any more heartache. I wanted to resolve my case as painlessly and as quickly as humanly possible. I wanted to give the opposition whatever they ask for to end the warfare. I even offered to say that I had shot Sean to make things easier on everyone involved. Both of my lawyers refused to allow me to lie about my exact actions in the incident. My attorneys insisted that I fight back for a just outcome. The next stop was another legal hearing for the reduction of my set bail.

During my bail reduction hearing the prosecutor gave a command performance in persuasive speaking. He highlighted the extremely aggravating events that revolved around my case. He further emphasized the facts of Sean's death without mentioning any logical reasoning or provocation for such a crime to take place. He even used my valid passport to show evidence of my plan to flee if I were given a lower bail, neglecting to add that my passport was over eight years old. Furthermore, he presented over fifty testimonials as to my character from people who ranged from lawyers, doctors, business owners, family members and friends.

The end result was that Judge Cornel denied bail reduction, as well as refusing to accept our plea for a ten percent bail of the total amount. He further dismissed our request to put up a combination of cash and property, which equaled over four hundred thousand dollars, in lieu of a two hundred thousand cash bail. My mother's wish was to raise the bail money and hand them to Judge Cornel, in rolls of pennies.

The next mind-blowing event was the media interviews with the prosecutor. Mr. Harrison, made an eloquent speech about how there are so many other ways to avoid abusive treatment. He spoke to the media firmly, announcing that I needed to be punished to the full extent of the law, given the fact that I was a successful business woman who had no need to take the law into her own hands, and offered a plea bargain which would substantially reduce my sentence.

Although they had no intention of prompting me to accept such a sentence, my attorneys were obligated to inform me of such an offer. This was another blow to my sense of hope. We decided to fight this prosecutor by getting the truth out to the public. This was achieved through media interviews given by my attorneys and my family members. My attorneys were convinced that pressure from the public would force the prosecutor to be more open-minded.

Fifteen

Prosecutorial Plea Game

Prosecutor Harrison was transferred to the New London County Prosecutors' Office a few months later. I was then assigned a new prosecutor Mr. Casidy who would prove to be much more open to the plea of extreme abuse and provocation which characterized my case. He immediately began bargaining with my attorneys for an agreement to settle on the basis of a more palatable sentence. Since we would save the taxpayer's dollars by not going to a drawn-out trial, a plea bargain was an incentive alternative. It also guaranteed that the state be rewarded a criminal conviction, as opposed to a trial judged by twelve individuals that could find me not guilty. It was called a win-win situation.

For the next ten months the legal authorities auctioned off years of my life, in exchange for an easier job. Deal after deal was brought to the table, gambling years of my life without the slightest consideration that any decision would be tethered upon my back for life.

Time was passing as I remained locked behind bars. Every day, for thirteen months, I slept, ate, drank, defecated, urinated, showered, and entertained myself within the confines of that small block unit. At times the smell of poorly ventilated air, combined with the aroma of unwashed bodies, coupled with cigarette smoke to created a stench so thick that it sometimes took my breath away. Due to overcrowding, women lay on the day room floor on mattresses, many of them drug addicted, and in the grips of withdrawal, endured seizures. It was my introduction to the street life Earth School 101, a terrible reality to watch.

Every morning the cleaning buckets would be pushed through the remote-controlled glass paneled doors, big industrial yellow pails with dirty cotton mops standing in mucky soapy water. There was no bleach to disinfect the area, because the officers were afraid that the detainees would either drink it or throw it at each other. I tried to get to the bucket first so that at least my cell would be somewhat clean. Otherwise, the water became so black that cleaning your cell with it would prove to be a useless chore. I eventually became the unit cleaning person as a job. Since, most of the other women being either mentally incompetent or locked downed for disciplinary actions, leaving me as one of the so-called normal detainees within that unit, the cleaning job was automatically given to me. I was paid one dollar a day. I also had the extra perk of being blessed with a state-issued pair of sneakers, which replaced my size eleven flip-flops. I was most grateful for the shoes and the semi-clean water.

The cards and letters arrived by the dozens, greetings from family members, friends, former clients, coworkers and complete strangers. I received books and journals to keep my mind clear and focused on the real world, something which was desperately needed. This reality check came from all of the written correspondence, personal visits and telephone calls home. My family kept me strong and my heart connected to their love. I had the memories of good times shared with my friends to push me into a happier place even if it was only for a moment. The strength of the human spirit surprised me as did the concern and support of the individuals who contacted me. These people helped boost my spirit, while my attorneys kept me grounded in hope.

The more the media spotlighted my case, the more mail came pouring into my cell including, letters of support from complete strangers. Some were accompanied with checks for my defense fund, but a few were from criminals who seemed to think that there was a bond between us. But I accepted this. I only wished that I had received some of this support when Sean was still alive. But I thought of him in a vague distant state of mind. It was as though I had known him in another lifetime.

In the interim, I remained focused on my notes. I searched the cobwebs of my mind for memories from as far back as I could remember, a difficult task since I had spent so many years living in an alternate identity. One of the reasons I was able to move forward in my life was due to my ability to shut out the past. I pushed it out of my mind so that I could thrive in a normal life. Digging back into the tragic events of my past was difficult, to say the least. I spent a full seven months in my cell writing down my life history at the request of my attorneys so that they could better serve my defense. And because they had to have all kinds of information about me from many different sources, they were truly amazed to learn of the numerous people who came forward in my defense. They even received several phone calls from former high school classmates, offering to testify on my behalf. They had present employees, and clients offering to do whatever they needed to assist in my defense. They hired a private investigator to go out into the field and interview people that knew me. The investigator confirmed all of the lead information I provided to them.

Ned and Jay both were further astounded to discover that a couple of people who had had a relationship with Sean had experienced must the same sort of abuse. My former girlfriend, Cookie, contacted my lawyers when she saw me on the local news channel and offered her help in my defense. She later wrote a detailed letter of the many ways that Sean had abused me back when we were teenagers, including the time when he, having locked me in the bedroom and threatened to kill me, had beaten me so badly that Cookie's boyfriend Donny had had to break through the door to help pull Sean off me. She revisited that memory with as much clarity as the day it occurred. I was surprised by the impact Sean's behavior had on other people. Cookie outlined his character traits and her statement turned out to be exactly the sort of thing Sean had said. I had written some of the exact same phases as Cookie. My attorneys held them side-by-side and were pleasantly amazed at the familiarity between the two.

Ned Mushin was so involved in different high profile cases that his attention was required elsewhere most of the time. That left Jay Jaron to do most of the footwork which included visiting with me almost daily until, as my case history became more and more complex, my attorneys had to hire another lawyer to join our defense team. Her name was Julie Warren Esq . . . A female defense attorney was warmly welcomed by me. She was incredibly understanding and sweet. I really appreciated her demeanor and her patience. We had an immediate understanding of one another. I felt, I discovered, that I was more comfortable telling a woman, as opposed to a man, intimate things about myself. In time, she became a key person in my world.

One of the individuals that contacted my attorneys to help was a former client named Sophia Tangelo. She had called my attorneys and offered her assistance with fund raising efforts or any other job they might have deemed necessary but didn't have the time to do. Sophia became a very essential part of my defense team and also a close and dear friend. She took on tasks of fund raising to helping collect information for my defense. She contacted people for my attorneys and did a lot of small jobs that they didn't have time for, as well as extending herself to my family and offering to help with the distribution of items from my house to things my daughter or my mother may have needed.

Over the lengthy time that I awaited trial and my mother grew more ill, Sophia took on more of a pivotal role in my life. She wrote me a private letter that outlined her personal experiences of an abusive relationship which explained how she felt compelled to reach out to me and offer help. Upping the ante, we tried to prepare ourselves for whatever punishment I was given. With a grateful heart and hopeful mind, I called Sophia my modern guardian angel. Each and every day I was locked away from society, I had Sophia's friendship.

Sometime in April 1994, a woman named Saddie Gross contacted my attorneys claiming to have been Sean's former wife, after he had left me. She told them that she had watched my case on the news and felt morally obliged to share the fact that he had been equally abusive to her.

Shortly following her communication, my attorneys acquired great confidence that my story was believable and real. They told me that the reason they ask me to write my history down was to verify its validity from other sources and now that they had an overwhelming influx of people telling them the same story that I told, they trusted me all the more. As lawyers they were always doubtful about what the accused communicated to them. It was just a matter of caution from experience. Their rule was to remain doubtful about what was told them until proven otherwise. Now, however, both of them agreed that I was telling them the truth. At that point they were confident enough to ask me to take a polygraph test to prove that I was not the person who shot Sean. This was a very risky move because, if I failed the test, the state of Connecticut would hold it against me. But, of course, my answer, without hesitation, was yes. I jumped at the opportunity to prove that I was telling the truth about the shooting ordeal.

Prosecutor, Mr. Casidy, insisted that, in order to commit to a reasonable plea agreement, he wanted the person who shot Sean to admit it on record. Otherwise, bargaining for a lesser sentence was off the table, so to speak. Mindy refused to admit she had shot Sean. This left me to prove my innocence in the actual shooting. Although I took full responsibility for Sean's death, I could not admit to an act that I did not commit. In my heart it did not lesson the fact that it was my fault he was killed. The sentencing for either would still remain equal in punishment. The prosecutor just wanted the shooter to announce to the public that they had committed that portion of the crime. This made my case harder to resolve. I had to prove this to them and a polygraph would supply that proof. I was excited to get this test on its way.

A few weeks later I met with a man named Glen Flynn who had been hired by my attorneys because he was a polygraph specialist. His credentials showed a vast variety of field expertise. He had served for over twenty-five years with the State Police Force and had become a private lie detector consultant after retirement in 1979. Prior to becoming a free agent in the community, Mr. Flynn had worked for the New York State Police as a polygraph commander at their headquarters in Bridgeport, Connecticut. During his fifteen years of private practice, he had worked for various defense attorneys as well, as a number of Fairfield County prosecutors offices, conducting all of the polygraph exams in homicide cases committed in Connecticut from 1979 until 1985 for the New York Prosecutor's Office. He also worked for the United States Treasury Department and U.S. Army and had testified as an expert witness in Municipal, Superior, and Federal Courts in Connecticut, New York and Vermont and had given testimony in over fourteen counties. He conducted over eight thousand polygraph examinations all related to criminal investigations.

Mr. Flynn met with me in an interview room at the county jail where he conducted his interview with me prior to administering the polygraph examination. Mr. Flynn was polite but had a demeanor that was reminded me of an investigator. He was professional and focused. He asks questions regarding my background and certain information regarding Sean's death to make sure that I was not under the influence of any medication.

Mr. Flynn then sat me in a plastic chair and began to attach many wires to different part of my body. Clipping a pulse measurement gauge to my finger, he told me to remain as still as possible throughout the testing period, and to answer every question with a simple yes or no. The large machine set on top of the table had long needle-like arms that continually moved up and down. As they scratched across the paper below, each one marked it with a check, moving in a rhythm congruent, with my body's response to each question. The time that elapsed since I was initially hooked up to the machine seemed like hours, but once the test was finished, Mr. Flynn informed me that he would review the charts and confer with my attorneys at a later time.

Mr. Jaron came to visit with me the following day and informed me that Mr. Flynn had reviewed the test charts, and after conferring with another experienced polygraph examiner, had determined that my answers were truthful and honest. The test results proved that I was not the person who fired the shots that killed Sean Donnelly. I finally had a glimmer of hope. It was the first time since my arrest that the truth had been revealed, and I was convinced that this would be the ingredient I needed to resolve this issue with the state's prosecutor.

As it turned out, however, it was not so cut and dry. Prosecutor Casidy was not satisfied with the results, because he had not hand-picked the polygraph examiner by himself, nor had the test been given at his suggestion or request. Of course my attorneys knew that the real reason Mr. Casidy was dissatisfied, was because the test results were not in agreement with his theory. Regardless of what the State's position was on this issue, I knew the truth was revealed and I took solace in that fact.

My attorneys had requested that Mindy be polygraph tested as well, and after two months of bantering back and forth with her attorney, it was agreed that she would summit to a polygraph examination. However, the test results were flawed because, during the examination, she became hysterical. A few weeks later she was given another polygraph test by the same examiner and this one also was recorded as inclusive. She was then given a third test administered by the same examiner in which the result was so slightly above inconclusive that it was considered as passing.

My attorneys were irate at the fact that the prosecutor had arranged three separate tests administered by the same examiner over and over again.

They were convinced that they would have given Mindy as many tests as it took, to arrive at the answer they desired, "a passing result". To refute this circus type behavior from the State's prosecutor's office, my attorneys offered to have me submit to another polygraph examination. This time, they let the prosecutor suggest whatever expert polygraph examiner the State and my attorneys agreed upon.

It was already October 10, 1994 by the time I was tested again by Mr. Karl Claus, an expert picked out and agreed on by the prosecutor Mr. Casidy. Mr. Claus, with forty-five years' experience as a polygraph specialist, determined that all of my answers were true and further wrote that, in his professional opinion, I had not fired either of the two gunshots that had caused Sean Donnelly's death.

After the conclusion of this polygraph evaluation, the prosecutor was left with two options: to accept the fact that I was not the person who fired the shots, or to drop the shooting issue completely which, after calling it a "moot point," he chose the latter. After ten months of the State demanding to have the identity of the person who actually shot Sean, he then changed his mind. This just added to the mountain of frustration my attorneys and I felt.

During the six months of trying to establish my innocence I encountered many other and personal issues that commanded my attention. My entire existence had become an endless stream of intense regret. Marie had been ripped from her home. Her familiar normal life had vanished completely and, having moved in with my family in Stamford, she was finding it difficult to fit in. The moment she stepped off of the bus on the first day of school, her peers taunted her. Marked with the ugly scar of having a mother accused of murder, she was teased and threatened to the point that it was too painful to attend, making it necessary for my mother to hire someone to home school her. She also underwent psychological counseling for the traumatic events she had been forced to endure.

My parents struggled with the emotional upheaval she presented to their household. Marie was rebellious because she was filled with the tremendous pain of my choices. I understood her emotions but my parents had too much on their plate to have such discord. Marie soon refused to comply with the new house rules. She fought my parents at every turn. At that point, my mother had suffered two strokes and was too weak to be a caretaker of an unruly teenager. When Marie and a young man whom she had been dating, who decided to run off to North Carolina together, my mother was powerless to stop her. It was not long after she left that we learned Marie was pregnant.

This new shock resonated through me as I realized that I didn't even know my own daughter anymore, causing me to fall into a deep depression even though I understood her need to have something she was connected to. This unborn baby would become something of her own. No one could take this child away from her. She felt as though the baby would fill the painful chasm inside of her. After all, her stepfather had abandoned her, her biological father had been killed and her mother was behind bars, possibly for life. She was stripped of everything, all the security she had ever known. It was an extremely sad state of affairs for everyone. With each day I was away from home, we grew further and further apart.

Throughout these months of uncertainty I was visited on a weekly basis by dedicated friends, including my stepfather, Ed, who became our family's anchor, making all financial decisions as my proxy, as well as arranging for the renting of my house in my absence, and buoying up my spirits, despite the fact that he had his own personal problems. He was, I often thought, an oasis of calm in my chaotic world which included the frequent shakedowns that occurred that winter and spring, during which I spent most my time submerged in legal preparation, writing for my attorneys, answering the massive amounts of mail from friends and family, reading books from novels to self-help and visiting with loved ones.

Numerous inspiring visits were with my two friends, Sophia Tangelo and Ron Holman. Sophia had become a forerunner in the inter-circle between my attorneys, my family and me, networking to keep people in support of my defense and managing to visit with me several times weekly. Sophia was my lifeline in this trying time. Our visits inspired me to go on fighting and to do so with vigor and valor. She always related to my every emotion I expressed, although some seemed earth shattering to me at the time, in the process, bringing me a new rationality which calmed me and kept me from jumping to conclusions. She had the ability to analyze each notch on the emotional scale, always able to bring to light more rational thinking and approach. She taught me to breath in the moment, center myself and think before I jumped to conclusions. All in all, just by being our natural selves, we balanced one another.

Sophia had taken my spontaneity example to another level when she decided to drive up to the prison compound. She and a friend tried to quell my anxiety by taking a look around the prison grounds, in the process missing the no trespassing sign and headed toward the entrance, only to be halted by an armed guard, innocently causing an upheaval at the front gate. In retrospect, we laugh at the ridiculous risk she had embarked upon.

My friend Ron Holman was another blessing, but on a spiritual level. I had known Ron for many years prior to this tragedy, his wife and I having become great friends while working together. He was a gentle, calm individual that dug deeply in the spiritual meaning behind every life occurrence. He always found something meaningful from a painful situation, and he taught me to do the same.

Ron actually looked forward to the life lessons that were given to him, nicknaming me "The Strong One," and himself "The Mentor". During one of his visits with me he told me that his soul was jealous of my experience, and that vicariously, through me, he would go on the journey. Ron truly did go on the entire journey with me, popping up whenever I needed a spiritual boost, sending me meditation books and spiritual writings which we would discuss on our next visit. I don't think that I realized, at the time, just how fortunate I was to have such unusual and caring friends.

SIXTEEN

Pre-Trial Confinement

DURING THE MONTH OF JUNE 1994, the televisions of America were tuned into the notorious police chase of the infamous OJ Simpson in his get-away Bronco. The media lit up the national spot light, directing everyone's attention on the murders of Nicole Brown Simpson and Ron Goldman, OJ Simpson being the police agency's number one suspect. O.J.'s dramatic get away, down the Californian freeway did not help to prove his innocence. In fact this horrifying murder would mark the beginning of the legitimate bargaining phase for my case since it brought to light the fact of many different economically diverse backgrounds being touched by domestic violence, and in so doing, broadened society's knowledge of the dynamics that encompass an abusive relationship. Even the legal system had been prejudged by the myths that surround the cycle of violence inflicted by a significant partner. The blatant truth was that society and judicial agencies viewed abused women, as being in the lower income status, with little to no financial resources to leave their abusive partner. OJ Simpson's case showed that violence could happen in the homes of the affluent as well.

As a result of the media attention in the OJ Simpson trial, my case became less abstract. To the public, it displayed a realism of the dramatic level of fatal possibilities to which the batterer could resort. As the OJ Simpson trial became a three-ring circus Americans were nevertheless outraged by the whole reality of violence in the home. They were especially perplexed to hear that a famous person could be guilty of a crime that they had been led to believe only happened in the homes of inner-city folks.

Certainly it was not supposed to involve a football hero living the "good life," a millionaire who won trophies for athletic excellence. Unfortunately, it became a race issue, as well. But the message was clear. Domestic abuse happens at every income level.

The prosecutor, in my case, a Mr. Casidy, was more than willing to avoid a full-blown trial since he envisioned the jury of my peers being more empathic to the provocation behind my crime and likely to find me not guilty. His focus turned instead toward a conviction through a plea bargaining agreement. My attorneys and the prosecutor's office met on several occasions and discussed plea considerations. Mr. Casidy wanted certain criteria met. In rebuttal, my attorneys demanded something from them in exchange. I learned over time that it became a bargaining game of wills and skills which involved the side that could hold out the longest and which side had the greatest amount of tricks up their sleeve. The best of show the one that held his bluff and stone poker face the longest was sure to win.

These skills were important in pushing the envelope for a better plea offer further. My attorneys had managed to bargain Mr. Casidy down to a twenty-five year sentence with a term of ten years served before parole eligibility. We continued to push for a lighter sentence, while my attorneys brought in the top forensic psychologist for battered women syndrome, in the United States. Stacy Fienstein M.D, a graduate from Yale University and published had an eleven-page booklet, which outlined her "curriculum vitae". Dr. Fienstein was the same psychiatrist that represented Lorraina Bobbit in the battered women syndrome case that had involved the severance of Mr. Bobbit's penis, as a way of ending her abusive martial rape.

Communications between my attorneys and Dr. Fienstein had been ongoing for weeks. She examined the facts surrounding my situation, and wanted to meet with my parents before she would consider taking my case, after which, hearing the stark facts, she agreed to take my case pro bono if I could pass a lengthy psychiatric examination.

The news of Dr. Fienstein acceptance of my case was thunderous. My family, friends, legal team and myself were elated at the implication of such a renowned forensic psychiatrist willing to come on board in my defense. Again, the glimmer of hope glowed inside me. It was these tiny sparks of hope that kept me together during such a stressful existence, even though it meant resurrecting painful memories, including that of my dysfunctional family.

Dr. Fienstein was amazingly small framed for an individual, with such powerful credentials and background, and she asked questions about my life experience from early childhood to the present, a process which took seven hours, after which she prescribed anti-anxiety medication.

Feeling as though I had just swum the English Channel, I returned to my concrete cell both exhausted and exhilarated. As painful as it had been to rehash every event in my life, it had also been a relief to voice them. My appreciation for the chance to have this highly qualified woman help me was overwhelming. Dr. Fienstein would be able to relay my experiences on a scientific level, one that would be explained so that people would understand the mechanics of my mindset. Hopefulness for a greater understanding was foremost in my mind.

My attorneys awaited my daily phone call. They seemed very optimistic of Dr. Fienstein's interview which they intended to present to the court at my sentencing hearing, after which they would plea leniency and a sentence reduction from eight to five years, based on her testimony in open court. That evening was one of the better nights I had experienced in the ten months spent in the County's Correctional Facility. For the first time, I had a tangible vision of surviving the upcoming judgment day. It had been a roller coaster ride for almost a year, but I finally had hope for my case to be presented as clearly as possible, a case based on the absence of any criminal history, together with the evidence of abuse, the character witnesses, the doctors testimony on Battered Women Syndrome, the law-abiding life I had led prior to the crime, the police reports, restraining orders, precautions for safety taken, and two polygraph tests.

However, a twist of fate changed my positive focus into one of despair. Upon calling home to tell my parents about Dr. Fienstein's interview, I was told that my mother had to have an emergency hysterectomy. She had suffered another mini stroke and the hospital had discovered a mass in her uterus which had to be removed immediately. She had suffered so much stress with my situation over the last year that I was convinced that all of that hardship caused her to have several strokes and now a tumor. My mind was plagued with my responsibility for yet another tragic occurrence.

Sentencing was set for December 16, 1994. I had clung to the hope that it would be reduced to the five-year mandatory term since I found myself unable to fathom an eight-year term with a total sentence of twenty-five years. The reality of that many years brought me to my knees. I prayed every day for a thunderous miracle to take place. A week before my day in court, my attorneys came to visit me. They had arranged a special visit with both my mother and stepfather during which they would be able to visit with me in person and not through the typical glass pane window. I was exhilarated at the thought of seeing my mother. She had only come up to see me once in the county jail, and had not been able to come again because she couldn't bear the experience of sitting in a glass encased booth. Although, I spoke with her every single day, I hadn't actually seen her with the exception of a few times outside my window, and in the courthouse. Her health had been waning over the year, and she wasn't strong enough to endure the emotional ramifications of a visit.

But as it turned out, I was naïve to think that we would be able to rejoice in a future in which we could all be together again, including my daughter who, carrying her own baby, had just returned from the Carolinas. It was wonderful to hold my mother in my arms again, but then my attorney Jay explained that my mother's ovarian cancer was terminal and that they had wanted me to hear the news before they introduced it as part of their plea for leniency in the courtroom.

Although I pretended to be brave in front of her, I cried until dawn, now completely convinced that I was solely responsible for my mother's terminal illness. Wave after wave of disappointment had eaten away at her physical wellbeing and was rapidly killing her. I was convinced that God was punishing me for the sins I had committed.

SEVENTEEN

Sentencing Hearing

I HAD BEEN AWAKE ALL night in anticipation of my Day of Judgment when the cascading light of dawn breaking against the earth's horizon came pouring through the grills of my jail cell window.

My mind focused on one still frame after another of the events of the past year as I paced my cell in anticipation of what awaited me, feeling as though every nerve ending in my body had been ignited. And yet all I could really think of was my daughter's fate. Sorrow consumed me as the pain I had caused so many people I loved overwhelmed me. Taking a deep breath and holding my head high, I pushed back the emotions that threatened to overwhelm me.

And then the time came. And because the judge had denied my lawyers' request that I appear in court wearing ordinary street clothing, I was led down the corridor dressed in an orange jump suit, my hands and ankles shackled. It was still another humiliation to be added on to the arrest, interrogation, arraignment, bail denial, bail appeal denial, prosecution measures, dirty tricks with phone taps, rearranged jail house witness setups, prearranged polygraph exams to bend the results in their favor, vague prosecuting attorney visits, media influence to tip the scales of justice and now a setup of my appearance in court to appear more monstrous to the public, by being forced to dress in a flame orange jumpsuit, with big bold black letters stamped across my back reading County Correctional Facility. It was all just a taste of our system's bell curve.

Upon entering the courtroom, despite being blinded by the flashing cameras and lights, my first thought was to look for my daughter and mother in a room in which people were packed like sardines, and found to my dismay, that they had been seated directly behind me so that I was only able to give them a loving nod before being seated, along with my lawyers, at a long table, facing the judge, a dramatic figure with long, silver grey hair, a man who gave the impression of enjoying the limelight.

After the brief opening arguments, Prosecutor Casidy spent four hours presenting the court with a crime which, according to him, had occurred without regard for human life, making a point of stressing the need for a severe punishment to serve as a deterrent, to others, and myself from committing other crimes. He contrasted the severity of the crime and the plea bargain agreement the state and my attorneys had agreed upon, after which one of my attorneys introduced the mitigating circumstances and evidence on my behalf, including the five books they had compiled as my sentencing memorandum. Those booklets contained my family history, facts of what lead up to the crime I had committed, letters of long term friendships for character reference, numerous letters pleading for leniency, my own personal letter to the judge, a letter submitted from Sean's former wife who had suffered great abuse, my two polygraph tests that proved beyond a doubt that I had not committed murder, and my psychological evaluation report conducted by forensic psychiatrist, Stacy Fienstein.

Unfortunately, after my attorneys presented the evidence on my behalf Judge Kline rebutted most of the testimony. The facts that so many law-abiding citizens were present and had written letters supporting me seemed to annoy The Honorable Kline. He acknowledged the support of the numerous individuals but responded by saying, "Although it is nice that so many influential people support Ms. Saunders, that sort of thing doesn't carry much weight in my courtroom."

The polygraphs test results were ignored completely because they are not considered legal evidence in a court of law. My attorneys informed me that if the results of those tests had been proven negative; then and only then, would they have validity. It all seems very one sided to me. All of the information I thought would aid in my defense seemed to create the opposite effect.

Ned introduced Dr. Stacy Fienstein and asked that Judge Kline allow her to testify on her expertise in the field of Battered Woman Syndrome. Dr. Fienstein would also share her professional fact-finding of my history of abuse and her opinion of the mechanics of why I acted in the manner I had. Judge Kline welcomed the doctor's testimony almost in an eerily condescending fashion.

Someone made a statement alluding to the fact that my defense team had paid for a renowned forensic psychiatrist to speak on my behalf when in truth Dr. Fienstein had volunteered to take on my case free of charge. This gracious woman never even asked for traveling expenses, although she had gone back and forth between Virginia to Connecticut on several occasions despite the fact that her time was extremely valuable. It was her belief in my life experience of abuse that prompted her to offer her expert testimony in open court. Ned rebutted the statement of Dr. Fienstein being a paid witness.

When Dr. Stacy Fienstein took the stand to give her formal report, she first stated her credentials and background certifications and then went on to speak of the dynamics of Battered Women's Syndrome and its mind conditioning effects after explaining that she had interviewed me for several hours. She went on to detail her scientific findings of the cause and effects that the abuse I had suffered had left on me. The Honorable Kline abruptly interrupted her mid-sentence in order to question the entire science of psychology, and Judge Kline began to give his opinion that psychology was not an exact science. He then turned toward the cameras with a smug expression and asked Dr. Fienstein if, in fact, it were. And although she agreed, she stressed the fact that the entire world still relies on psychological findings to determine the state of mental health for individuals.

Dr. Fienstein continued her professional evaluation result of the fact that I suffered from Battered Women Syndrome. Again Judge Kline interrupted her summary with yet another question, wanting to know if, in fact, most psychological findings are based on information given to them by the individual and when she relayed that that was so, stated that the subject she was evaluating might well have lied, to which she replied that, although that could be the case, it was up to the expertise of the examiner to determine what was truth, and what was not. She continued to explain that a professional examiner is trained to detect these occurrences. Dr. Fienstein kept her professional composure throughout each interruption questioning the validity of her profession and continued to relate my actions to that of a person suffering from Battered Woman's Syndrome.

The Honorable Judge couldn't resist another inquiry. Having stated that he had studied Battered Woman Syndrome, he declared that, in his opinion, most Battered Women did not strike back at their abuser and continued with a summation of the most common behaviors of abused women. Dr. Fienstien agreed that it was not commonplace for most battered women to strike back at their abuser, but that that didn't mean that it never happened. Dr. Fienstein continued to testify that I was a clear textbook case of a woman, who suffered from Battered Women Syndrome. She further explained that my level of mental perception of hopelessness, coupled with the chain of events had prompted me to act on those realistic fears and strike back at Sean.

With every interruption from Judge Kline my body froze, and my stomach tightened to think that he could refute the entire testimony of such a renowned forensic psychiatrist, speaking to this professional as if she had just graduated from a local high school. I felt saddened that the judge obviously had every intention of refuting her clinical findings. However, I had a greater sense of pure embarrassment for Judge Kline's condescending behavior toward her.

The Honorable Judge graciously obliged my defense attorneys' requests in presenting my case, only to contradict him whenever possible strategically making statements or posed questions contradicting our legal argument. Otherwise, he was impassive almost to the point of being sarcastic. I was convinced that he was soaking up the camera exposure. I felt as though the courtroom was a backdrop for a Broadway show, and the Honorable Judge had the leading role. My heart told me that the ending of this play would be final curtains for me. Certainly it was not a chance for a new beginning.

I felt as though I was trapped inside a tunnel, their voices fading away. It was the only way of enduring this three-ring circus. My palms sweat so much that I managed to mangle an entire box of tissues that Julie had handed to me one by one. Hot salty tears streamed down my cheeks. And since it was almost impossible to wipe them from my face with my hands cuffed and tied to my waist, I constantly contorted my body in a crunch like position in order to dab the tissue to my eyes.

I was abruptly drawn back to reality when Dr. Fienstein left the stand. Judge Kline was speaking but his words were jumbled, swirling around in my head. I kept thinking that this was another failed attempt to present any understanding of my case. So many questions popped into my head. Did anyone in this room, aside from me see through this staged production? Was it me or was this really happening? Did anyone notice how Judge Kline was addressing the court? Was Judge Kline only concerned with media attention? Whatever the answers to these questions, I knew this was not going to end well.

My attention drifted in and out during the proceedings, my only option being to endure what was happening. After my attorneys completed their mitigating evidence, Prosecutor Casidy presented the aggravating factors, presenting all of the horrible details of the crime. Hearing the events, without reasons for how such a crime would be committed, did leave a horrific mental photo for everyone in the room. Aggravating evidence consisted of the hard, cold facts, without reference to my emotional and physical torture. Hearing just those facts made for easy consideration for a conviction of the maximum measure. Punishment would be easy to impose after hearing his colloquy. I sat at that defense table completely overwhelmed with a sinking feeling of doom.

My attorney presented the courtroom, filled with people who supported my plea for leniency, with the hard, cold facts. He reiterated that I had a promise of employment upon my release which showed that I would be a contributing member of society as a productive individual. Ned showed the court proof of the community ties I was connected to as a positive factor and went to claim that my family background was rife with continued cycles of abuse before pointing out the direct systematic correlation of my grandfather and my paternal father's battering behaviors, connecting them to my acceptance of such behaviors. He explained that a young person in such an environment learned to view abuse as normal ingredients in a relationship. Ned visited the fact that my daughter has continued the pattern of dysfunctional partnership with her current boyfriend and addressed the fact that she sat in the courtroom in her second trimester of pregnancy with her abusive partner's child. Ned stressed that Marie was in desperate need of her mother.

The following hardship presentation was just as painful as the first, relating as it did to my mother's terminal uterine cancer. Ned begged the court to grant my family the opportunity to have me home at an earlier date, touching on the fact that the crime I had committed was an aberrational incident and that I posed no threat to society, explaining that I was a fearful, desperate person that had panicked under reasonable and real fear. He further, expressed my sincere remorse for the death of Sean and that I took full responsibility for my actions in this criminal act. Ned stated that, although I was not the person that had shot Sean, I fully accept the blame for his death. He relayed that I had voluntarily taken, not one but two polygraphs exams and passed both. Two separate polygraph examiners had administered the test and they both concluded that, when ask if I had shot Sean, I had truthfully answered no. Ned concluded his summation with another plea for mercy from the court on my behalf.

Sean's mother Dawn was next to voice her peace. She cried out that her son was a sick individual that didn't deserve to die. She also accused me of having killed him and went on to say that she and her family had been getting him help for his drug and alcohol addictions. And then, pointing at me, she went on to say that I had a drug problem and that I had been jealous of Sean. I was stunned with her attack, along with her summation of reasons. I was certainly taken back by her words and her overall demeanor. My first thoughts were an influx of different memories of Dawn during the time we tried to get Sean help. I distinctly remembered the evening that both of her sons were having a bloody Irish brawl. Dawn was screaming for Sean and me to run from the house, before his brother Hank smashed his face in any further. On the way out of the front door Dawn said, "I gave birth to two monsters! "I then thought about my own child and the love I held for her. I looked back at my daughter Marie, and instantly felt sorry for the pain I caused her. I understood that she had to struggle to find reasons why I had behaved as I had, placing blame on her son. She continued to paint a picture of Sean as being a weak, sick individual that needed help. When she was finished speaking, she turned and faced my daughter and with great anger in her voice, shouted, "I'm sorry Marie"! I didn't know how she had come up with her reasons, other than abuse, for wanting Sean dead, but I attributed it to her denial and inability to look at the painful truth. I figured that looking at the truth would be similar to looking into the mirror. That is difficult for most people to do, even when the stakes weren't as high as the current situation. Dawn's memory to her son's life was incredibly sad.

Sean's brother Hank had not appeared in court that day. Hank's absence is still a mystery. If I had to guess I would say that there must have been some discord between Hank and the rest of the family because he had played a helpful role in my early defense. He extended information for my defense to my attorneys. Perhaps he was afraid he would be called up as a witness if he were present in court that day. No one will ever know the exact reason for his vacant seat. Actually, the only people in the courtroom who testified on Sean's behalf were his mother, sister and a few relatives totaling five individuals.

The court hearing continued to linger on what seemed like a lifetime. Judge Kline addressed the court with a lecture on Battered Women Syndrome and his understanding of such. He acknowledged that I suffered abuse at the hands of Sean, mistakenly referring to me by name and then calling me "the victim". Although each time he quickly corrected himself, he did this on three occasions. Judge Kline's reference to me as a victim would fuel me to fight for years to come. I held on to those words, using them as a life raft, a spark of hope to get me through many rough times.

Judge Kline then touched upon the aggravating factors in the case and the fact that he felt that it was necessary to set a punishment severe enough to serve as deterrence to others in order to avoid what he called "copy-cat crimes". He had a definite problem with what he referred to as "vigilante behaviors" or actions.

The complexity of my case grew with the lengthiness of my court hearing. Mindy sat in silence at the table adjacent from mine, her attorney holding onto a fifteen page-sentencing memorandum as he waited his turn. After a brief dissertation from Mindy's attorney, our fate was about to be announced.

Judge Kline instructed us both to rise. He briefly stated that we had both agreed to a plea bargain of twenty-five years with a mandatory minimum of eight years before parole eligibility for the crime of aggravated manslaughter. He further stated that, under the aggravating and mitigating circumstances, he was in agreement and thus satisfied with the prosecutors' plea offer. Although my attorneys had given it all they had to have the sentence reduced to a five-year term, Judge Kline was clearly about to crush any hope for leniency.

When the judge asked me if I had anything to add before he announced my sentence. I apologized to Sean's family and my own. I added that Sean had hurt me and that I felt that I had had no other choice for survival. The judge then asked me the million-dollar question, "Did you shoot Sean?" My answer was an immediate, "No, I did not shoot Sean. Mindy shot him for me," going on to state that, even though Mindy shot Sean for me, I was responsible for his death. Judge Kline then turned his attention to Mindy and asked the very same question. Instead of responding, Mindy stared straight ahead as though dazed. The judge again posed the question, and Mindy turned to her attorney and mouthed, "What do I say?" and when he told her to answer the judge's question, Mindy turned and whispered, "No, Margo did."

The courtroom was silent for what seemed to be a lifetime. Until finally the judge delivered a polemic about how unfortunate it was to end a criminal hearing without the clear cut truth of who exactly was responsible for Sean' death. He further stated that it did not hold any bearing on sentencing for the crime because the Connecticut law gives the shooter and her accomplice the same length sentence, and that we had both taken responsibility for Sean's death.

Every single person in that courtroom, including myself, was on the edge of his or her seat waiting for the judge to render his decision.

"Margo Saunders you are sentenced to a term of twenty-five years, with a mandatory minimum of eight years before parole eligibility. You will immediately become a ward of the State of Connecticut, to be held at the Connecticut State Correctional Facility in East Lyme, Connecticut to serve that term."

At that moment all the blood seemed to leave my body, and turning, I saw the despair in my mother's eyes. December 16, 1994 marked sentencing day for both of us. My mother's sentence was terminal cancer, and at that moment, my sentence, whatever it might be, felt just as terminal.

EIGHTEEN

Prison Confinement

IT WAS STILL DARK OUTSIDE as I was shuffled to the awaiting van for my hour and a half journey, emotionally broken and still in a state of disbelief to be transported to the Connecticut State Correctional Facility in East Lyme where I would serve my eight year sentence, riding in a van that was basically equipped with two long benches and a floor to ceiling wire cage that separated the two sides. And to my dismay, I was soon to be joined by convicted male inmates, all like myself shackled and handcuffed.

And then, finally, there was Mindy. With the exception of our court hearings, this was the first time since our arrest that we had been that close since we had been on a separation status our entire stay at County Correctional Facility. I never uttered a word to her the entire trip to prison, although there were so many questions that I wanted to ask her, the first and foremost being why she had shot Sean for me. Lord knows I had my theories, but I would never know for sure. Had she thought, as she had stated in one of her letters, that once I was incarcerated, Marie would become her child? Why had she played the part of this innocent girl who had been manipulated by me to commit this crime? Aware as I was of her delusional behavior of the past year in confinement, my final decision was never again to speak to her. What was the point of speaking at this stage in time? Even when the men disembarked at their destination, Mindy and I did not even look at one another.

It was dawn that winter's morning with the cloudy sky adding an extra chill to the icy steel fortress when the van stopped. I watched as an officer used a mirror mounted to a long pole with wheels attached, to check the undercarriage of the van. Paperwork was exchanged, leaving us locked between two gates, waiting for the front steel barricade to slide open. Minutes seemed like hours until the approval was given and the gates of my fate rolled aside. I had arrived at the maximum prison compound, and that was the last time I would come into close contact with Mindy Molee. For the rest of our stay at this institution, we were placed in separate housing units.

Following a strip search which, although conducted by a female officer, left me feeling as violated as though I had been raped, I was then taken to an intake unit, what the prison called reception-housing area. It was a very odd name for it because, to me, it was the furthest thing from receptive, containing as it did metal bunk beds, steel picnic tables, and an open shower section, beyond which, with no protective wall, were lines of toilets. This was the moment when I realized that we were expected to perform the most intimate bodily functions in the open for everyone to see.

Much of the routine I was now to encounter was familiar, but there were differences. The food was as appalling as that to which I thought I had become accustomed and the menacing stares from the new inmates, accompanied by the clinking of the matron's keys produced the same desire on my part to stay in my top bunk forever. There were orientation sessions in which we learned, among other things, the system by which sixty women could use the two phones available, and the ways we could use—and by implication—misuse the commissary system. The most important difference was, I found, the way in which these women, all of whom had been found guilty of serious crimes, tended to group together in ethnic units. And since I was not only Caucasian but also presumably guilty of the most serious crime of all, one would have thought that I would have felt right at home. But on the contrary, I felt even more alien than ever, surrounded as I was by hard-bitten criminals. I had, without a doubt, entered another dimension.

I was, I soon found, completely out of my element. All the surroundings and the individuals around me clearly came from a different world than I. My fear was that I wouldn't make it in this institution for good reasons. From the top of my bunk I looked around and thought about the fact that this could be my home for the next eight years. On December 2001, I would be eligible for parole and from this moment on until then, I vowed that I would dedicate myself to holding onto my own reality. My family and friends would be my bridge to sanity and my real life which I would rejoin one day. I kept telling myself that this nightmare was temporary and that I would overcome and rise above it. My body might be forced to remain in this place, but my heart and mind remained at home, my real home in the free world. I decided to grab each and every memory of my past and bathe in it, realizing that it was my only chance of survival. I figured out quickly that if I were to make it out of this place intact, I had to remain strong and show a fearless face. Each step would be a process toward the bigger prize, which was my freedom, and a reunion with all those who had supported me through the dark days of imprisonment which I had already endured.

In the meantime, I must learn how to get along with women who had long since worn out the support of their families and friend.

Most of the residents were Black Americans or Hispanics. The remaining, Caucasians for the most part, had a distinctly worn out look to them, sort of rough around the edges if you will, most of them having lived through years of drug and alcohol use. There was nothing polished about them. It was evident that many were former prostitutes, junkies and petty thieves who returned to the facility on a regular basis, their life styles leading them, inevitably, to the world of more serious crimes. Among their criminal offenses were, aggravated assaults, robbery, larceny, theft, drug trafficking and other related crimes. In some cases these crimes had led to homicides connected with felonies. A various number of inmates had never held a legitimate job. Most of the women were unable to read and write anything but their own name and had given birth to multiple children fathered by different men, children who were likely to end up in prison themselves someday. Given the number of inmates of this caliber, it was clear to me that, unless I was careful, I would be taken advantage of.

It helped that my heart was home with my family. My daughter was pregnant and a couple of months away from delivery, and although I would not be there for her in body, I would be with her in heart and mind. Still, I felt as if I had somehow failed her, as well as the rest of my family and that perspective tore me apart. She was sixteen years old, pregnant and alone in the world without parents, or anyone who was really bonded to her.

My mother who, under normal circumstances, could have been relied on to care for Marie was extremely ill with cancer of the uterus, too weak by now to fulfill that role, and although she was the family rock, it was inevitable that she should crumble before our eyes. I felt so guilty for her illness, certain that my life choices had played a role in making her sick. The belief that I had somehow caused her cancer was another burden that I was forced to assume, another burden I would place upon myself. Still, I used her strength to forge through. My heart said that if my mother could endure this ugly fate so could I conquer mine. I wanted her to be proud of my ability to rise above my captivity.

And through it all, she never faltered. Unable to write with her right hand, she sent me a left-handed scribbled message on a prayer card. The messages were reminders always to remain hopeful and strong regardless of what life had in store for you. It took such tremendous effort to write this to me that I carried it with me throughout my incarceration. Whenever I felt weak, I pulled out one of those messages and read it over and over again until I felt strong enough to hold my head up again. To this day, tears flood my cheeks while reading these precious documents.

Although time passed monotonously enough, on the whole, one other prisoner caught my attention because of her unusual appearance. Heavy breasted and over six feet tall, she had shaved herself as bald as any man I had ever seen. Likewise, she had adopted a man's swagger and associated almost exclusively with other women who, via their dress or demeanor, appeared to be as masculine as possible. These women embraced this look, as I was to discover, because it beneficial to them financially. It seemed that, since most of these women had exhausted any outside sources of income through family and friends, they used their hard exteriors to either trick some lonely females into thinking they were indeed men, or frighten other women into giving them items they demanded. Some of these women were actually prostitutes in the real world. They came to prison and shaved their heads to scam others. It was entirely a facade in order to survive inside prison walls. This facility held some of the highest level of master manipulators I have ever seen gathered in one place. Out of the sixty inmates sandwiched into the reception area, there wasn't one I felt any connection with.

Each and every evening like clockwork, at shower time, the officer would call out aisle rows according to our bed location, whereupon everyone lined up dressed in a facility-supplied flowered robe and shower slippers, along with our small white towel and our personal shower items before, five at a time, standing side by side, we used in the five minutes allotted to clean ourselves. Actually five minutes was more than long enough if one or more of your companions was one of the prisoners posing as a man, and as such, was eyeing you with an intensity that was as much a violation as it would have been had they actually been someone of the opposite sex.

During my three weeks of living in this commune, I became physically ill from constipation. There was something about having to relieve myself in an open area bathroom facility that instantly turned my bowels to concrete. I tried to sneak into the toilet area during the day when it was not so busy, but if there was any sign of people moving, my body froze up. It was involuntary interruption of all internal movement. For days I endured with tremendous pain in my intestines from the waste that had built up. It was evident that, when it came to defecating in public, I had stage fright.

All of the detainees were given three smoke breaks and a sixty minute exercise time in the maximum security exercise yard, a space consisting of both grass and concrete areas, which were sandwiched in between the two maximum-security buildings, one named Madison and the other Pierce Hall. I would measure the size of the yard to be about a quarter size of a football field. The entire compound was surrounded by a double fence, which was topped with razor wire sharp as a freshly honed tool.

From the very beginning, I noticed that most of my fellow inmates were fully aware of my well-publicized case, something that helped and hurt my integration into this facility. It helped me because inmates had a strange respect for individuals that were sentenced to long-term commitments, especially those prisoners that had committed crimes of a violent nature. On the other hand, it hampered my adjustment into prison, because the other women were well aware of my weaknesses when it came to personal relationships. I had been in an abusive situation of one sort, and now I was in another since prison can be an extremely predatory environment, one in which my past left me wide open to be preyed on. And since I was well aware of the fact that I was vulnerable to my surroundings, they scared the hell out of me, particularly since my idea of prison came not from direct experience, but by way of television and movies. However, ironically enough, my ignorance gave me a protective layer, so I worried less. At times, I found myself relieved that I was surrounded by well-armed officers and this aided me in my prison transition.

I occupied my spare time with writing letters to my loved ones, and organizing the little property I had been allowed to take with me. Photographs of my family and friends kept me focused on a reality I had once lived, giving me hope for a life I would have again. And each week, phone time helped me regain a piece of my real existence. Those precious moments gave me peace and hope to carry through from day to day, until we would speak again. It saddened me to hang up the receiver at the end of our conversations. Just hearing their voices pierced my heart, each phone call bittersweet. I rejoiced in hearing the comfort of their voices, and my heart sank as my phone time came to an end.

Whenever I exhausted my memory bank of the different life-saving good times I had once experienced, I began reading my inmate handbook. The handbook was, indeed, my bible. The rules and regulations were varied and detailed. For any minor infraction there was a punishment of being restricted to your bunk for up to ten days, during which you lost all privileges. For major punishment an inmate was detained in a segregated lock unit, which was located in a special isolation wing, within the institution. If the institutional sentence were longer than thirty days, the detainee would be transported to a segregation unit located at one of the men's prison facility. These major infractions would also effect a prisoner's good time accumulated for time spent confined. Thus losing good time meant losing credit of days rewarded for good standing. Good time was given according to the sentence imposed and how long you lived in maximum and in minimum units. If a sentence imposed was long enough, it could take years off of the totality of years actually spent behind bars.

Good time also had a great effect on an inmate's maximum and minimum status. In the case where an individual lost good time it made their total sentence longer, especially time spent in maximum-security housing. These infractions also greatly affected a person' parole release evaluation. The due process in the institution was to be served with a written charge. Depending upon the severity of the infraction, it would be either a pink sheet for minor, or a blue charge for major infractions. A higher-ranking officer such as a sergeant or lieutenant served the blue documents. After receiving the appropriate paperwork, you awaited an inner-institutional hearing. At such a hearing, the case was heard by an outside hearing officer, who was designated for each correctional facility.

Prior to the hearing, you could be interviewed and represented by an inmate paralegal representative who had been trained during their sentence. If the inmate were found guilty, the punishment would ensue immediately. Inmates that were accused of an assault, escape or any violent offense would be held in the detention lock-down unit while awaiting their hearing. Some of the major offenses included outside criminal accusations. If that were the case, the inmate would have to appear in court for adjudication of the criminal charge. Criminal charges such as escape would be heard in the Superior Courts.

The punishments for these offenses would be served at the conclusion of the prison's current sentence so that, legitimately, a prisoner could extend her sentence years beyond whatever the previous sentence imposed was originally. I was both intrigued and frightened by all the rules and regulations of this new world I had entered. And since the last thing I wanted was to spend one more second in this terrible environment. I decided to follow this book by the letter which was, as this example demonstrates, often difficult.

Three nights prior to my move into a more permanent living environment I was urinating in the public toilet area where a fellow inmate was crammed under the sink area in front of me, smoking a forbidden cigarette. When she offered me the butt and asked me to flush it, I saw no harm in doing so, only to find myself targeted by a correction officer who the inmate had obviously seen coming. Ending up as a scapegoat, was my first lesson of just how things worked in the prison world, although in this case, I was lucky enough to receive only a minimum punishment for a minor infraction of the rules.

NINETEEN

Maximum Security

AS A RESULT OF MY penalization involving the cigarette, I arrived at the Pierce Hall gate for my next housing unit assignment. This was my second trip to that building and hopefully my last for a while. The two female officers in my new unit reminded me of female police officers in television show. One was a tall blonde with a quiet but stern exterior. The other officer, whose demeanor was similar to that of a mischievous child, was shorter with dark hair. And from the moment I met them, I was assured that I had been sent to a better place. I was assigned a bed in a dorm unit that accommodated a total of eight women. As each woman before me moved forward to a higher level, they would change to an available bed in the smaller dorm which held four beds. After each inmate moved through that unit, one at a time, according to who arrived first, the next unit was a single private cell. I hungered for a private cell, a seven by ten feet slice of peace. I had my eye on the prize in this rotation.

The moment I walked into the eight-woman dorm and saw two other women, I felt the hair on the back of my neck rise. One was a thin, tall, light skinned black girl who, because of her cropped Afro, appeared at first glance to be a man with a chipped front tooth and a scar on her face that stretched from the corner of her mouth all the way to her temple. When I heard her companion call her Sam, I sensed that she was trouble, a premonition that seemed to be rapidly on its way to being realized when the other woman asked me if I was gay. When I replied that I certainly was not, she informed me that I soon would be. My mind went wild as I thought about the possibility of being assaulted, but I unpacked, telling myself to play it cool, and focus on the pluses, one of which was the fact that the showers here appeared to be separated.

Sam followed me around like a ravaging dog. Clearly she had a plan in mind for me, perhaps to serve as her avenue to free commissary items. I found out later that Sam was the institution's thorn, incorrigible in every way. There was an incident prior to my arrival at the facility that involved her setting fire to one of the maximum-security mental health units, after which she was serving her time here in Pierce Hall and given an outside criminal charge for arson.

This was not the first time Sam had been in trouble and it would not be the last. I overheard a few officers refer to Sam as the "She Devil". As bad luck would have it, I was assigned to the same unit as she. Sam viewed me as a rich white girl or cracker a reference to my ethnicity. Her behaviors were similar to that of a tiger in the jungle. She locked her eyes on the fresh kill, and I was it. Familiar with my past addiction to abuse, she used that information to her advantage. She was nice to me at first and then, at other times, was quietly threatening. I felt as though I was saved from one abusive situation only to be thrown into another since, once she had claimed her hunt, all of the other inmates backed away from bothering me.

I was soon made well aware of Sam's blatant hatred for white people which was a relief on the one hand since it indicated that she had no sexual interest in me and soon came to view her as somebody who would protect me, more willing to accommodate her need for monetary items then to be subjected to all the other prison predators within the facility.

My family and friends were permitted to send me clothing, personal items and food through the mail. They were also allowed to bring cooked food with them on a visit, the limit being fifty pounds a month. As they came to visit, the food was inspected for contraband and forwarded to my housing unit following the visit. My friends Sophia and Meg were frequent visitors and generous contributors to all my needs. Other individuals' friends, former co-workers and family members also sent me stamps, money orders, music tapes, and inspirational liturgy.

It was so refreshing to finally wear normal clothes after a year of wearing an orange jumpsuit. All of the clothing was stamped with our last name and inmate number. We had a limitation on each article of clothing. Summer clothing was sent home and winter clothing was sent in to replace them. As for the food, it was sheer delight and I savored each bite of the specially cooked delicacies my loved ones brought to me. In our unit there was a small kitchen where our meals were served three times daily. In between those meals, the officers would call refrigerator movement at which time we could go and retrieve our perishable food from the refrigerator, and use the microwave to heat it up. Everything was locked up tight, and our names were clearly written on each bag.

I was assigned a job in the facility's sewing factory. The sewing room was located in Madison Hall where I went to work every day at eight in the morning. Inmates earned different wages for a particular job. The sewing room was one of the lowest paying jobs, a five day a week deal for which I was paid just under thirty dollars a month. Every prisoner also received work credits for their assigned job, as well. The work credits allocated would actually reduce an inmate's total sentence. Certainly it was better to have a full seven days a week position than a shorter five days, but I was perplexed at the fact that I had an education and a trade and yet, I was given a job in a sewing factory.

The next morning I rose at six. After waiting in line for the bathroom facility, I prepared for breakfast, the only meal that was worth eating since there wasn't much you can do to mess up a hard-boiled egg and banana, although, the oatmeal and scrambled eggs were questionable. That day, as I was devouring my breakfast, I notice an inmate named Rhonda, at the next table putting hard-boiled eggs in her bra, no doubt saving them for a snack later on in the day. Unfortunately, on this morning, she was one of the prisoners randomly chosen for a pat down but since, apparently, the eggs weren't delicious enough to warrant a pink sheet charge, Rhonda was assigned to spend three days confined to her private room for punishment, a room she rarely left anyway. Rhonda was a fifty-year-old Caucasian woman who was sentenced to a fifteen-year mandatory minimum term for killing her husband whom she had shot in the groin after finding him in bed with his mistress. His penis and testicles no longer in existence, he died from the shotgun trauma. Basically, she only came out of the seclusion of her cell for meals and family visits.

Everything in this facility was on a timed schedule. Being late for a movement was unacceptable and resulted in an institutional charge, and so every morning I marched out of the dorm door to Madison Hall in a line with other prisoners like herded sheep without looking back, and since I had never been in a sewing facility before, it appeared to me like something out of a movie with machine after machine lined up next to one another, all of them manned by women sewing men's boxer shorts. The fact that the men's prison made all the women's clothing seemed a little backward to me, but I later learned that by doing so, it cut down on theft. I couldn't imagine anyone in his or her right mind wanting to steal institutional clothing, but it happened.

Having been assigned a sewing table in the middle of the room, I looked around to see that all of the inmates were being given scissors and felt instantly alarmed since there were only two unarmed guards which didn't seem very safe, particularly since several of these women were sentenced to life imprisonment for murdering someone.

Directly next to me was young Asian girl who talked incessantly in broken English the entire morning long. By the time we had broken for mid-morning count, Kim told me that god blesses me about ten times. I thought she was a little odd, but she seemed real sweet until a Spanish inmate told me to watch out for her, especially with scissors since rumor has it that she cut up her entire family in a massacre-killing spree. I kept my eyes open after that, although I'm not sure whether I was more surprised by that than the fact that someone in a position of authority had put someone with Kim's background in a room full of sharp objects.

Surprisingly, however, during the several months that I worked in the sewing room there was only one incident of violence involving a black woman with the nickname Pops, a woman with light brown skin and long brown dreadlocks, who worked two rows in front of my worktable. Her current criminal charge was that of the second homicide she had committed in her lifetime. Usually she wasn't a troubled inmate unless someone started an altercation with her. On this day, when another inmate started mouthing off to her from across the room, Pops jumped over the first row of sewing tables, scissors in hand, and had to be restrained first by an oversized correctional officer and then with others, armed with shields and clubs, who threw her to the floor and handcuffed her.

I have to say that I was crouched down under my sewing table in case others join in and was so petrified about having to go back into that sewing room again that someone in authority must have taken pity on me, with the result that I was given an interview with the head of the cosmetology program, a man name Al Carbucca who taught the beauty program out in the minimum-security section of the prison. I was elated to be saved from the dreaded sewing factory, and this job came with an extra perk, being labeled, as it was, a para-professional position for which I was paid three dollars a day. Life was beginning to seem a bit easier for me at the "Big House."

During the time of my transition in the prison system, it was not surprising that the media continued to be interested and I was not astonished when my attorneys notified me that one of the local New York television talk shows were interested in interviewing me. My lawyers and I agreed that it would be a good time to get my version of what happened out to the public. Since there were numerous mixed stories of what actually occurred in my case, I desperately wanted to tell my story as it happened. I felt that it would help other women that were in my situation, as well as, squash all the jumbled versions of what really transpired. My attorney assured me that this man, Willard Thomas, who hosted the show, would relay my story just as it was told. I was both excited and nervous to have this taped interview. My attorneys set up the taping of the show with the approval of the prison facility.

The interview was set up to take place in one of the classrooms in the Madison Hall building where, on one early morning, I nervously faced my interviewer, who seemed to be a likable, friendly man. The cameramen were busy setting up special lights and backdrops, closely monitored by prison officials because of the security issues within the facility, particularly since the hallways and gates could not be shown along with other security breaches that would compromise prison security.

The interview began unrehearsed. Mr. Thomas's questions were candid and direct, and I gave honest answers. After the first five minutes of the taping, I actually forgot about the cameras pointing at me. It was a welcome opportunity to have the camera aimed directly at me in a light that I was comfortable with, as opposed to the flashing and clicking of photographers in a courtroom setting.

The entire interview took about two hours. It was surprisingly painless. I felt comfortable speaking with this man. In fact, it was therapeutic to talk about the reasons why I was in such a terrible circumstance. I was relieved after the interview. It had been cathartic to purge myself of all that had happened to result in a crime based on self-defense. It showed that, although my criminal choice was wrong, the events leading up to the crime was completely reasonable, and made more sense of how such a terrible thing could occur.

When the television show aired, the entire prison population watched it. I have to say that I was satisfied with how my story was displayed. It made me feel good to share my story with others, to let them know the truth. I respected Willard Thomas and the television station that aired it.

A year and a half later, however, that the very same television station aired my interview again, this time displaying what had happened in an entirely different light. They labeled the show, "The Most Notorious Female Killers," and edited it in manner that emphasized the bloody nature of the crime without including any background explanation. There was not even the overriding theme of the abused woman. In other words, the media had completely bastardized the facts in a frenzied attempt to gain sensational ratings. Worse still was the fact that I had no legal recourse since I had signed away all rights to the footage.

Looking back, I realize how fortunate I was to have weathered the storm of an eight-bed dorm without bodily harm, Sam having kept all of the other inmates away from me. I didn't mind spending a few dollars in commissary items to have that peace. In prison the minute someone befriends another it is rumored that they are girlfriends. I didn't care what the others thought or whispered just as long as I was safe. The good part of it all was that, with my move to the four-man dorm, I would be located on a different wing in the building away from Sam which made it more difficult for anyone to attempt to take advantage of me. Furthermore, I was the next in line to move into my own room. I had never wanted seclusion so badly in my life.

An inmate had four possible options: to be restricted to the grounds, released completely after serving the full sentence, transferred back to their own country to await deportation or taken to the lock-down for punishment. I am ashamed to say that I wished for any of the above options in return for the peace and safety of my own cell, one which I was finally allotted in a quiet section of Pierce Hall where there were about eleven private rooms, a laundry room, three separate stall shower facility, a telephone mounted on the wall near the grill gate and a closet for cleaning mops which, given my situation in general, was as close as I could get to paradise complete with a new job as a hair stylist and a private room. This was the beginning of my upgraded stay at state prison and I proceeded to make my life a little more comfortable by ordering a television, clothing iron, hot pot, blow dryer, cassette player, ear phones, pens notebooks, and last, but not least, an electric word processing typewriter, all of which gave me a sense of control. As soon as I was situated in my own room, I rarely attended any institutional meal with the exception of breakfast and was soon able to lose Sam since, now that I had the sanctity of my own room, she was unable to access me without my consent. My job as the unit hairdresser was by appointment only.

Then, too, there was the fact that my room was located directly behind the officer's protective cage. It was a perfect situation for me. I didn't have to go on morning movements. I went to the end of my wing when my appointment was scheduled, and after the officer took out her large iron key, and opened the wing' gate, I walked across the hall to my designated room which was equipped with a shampoo sink and a barber chair. The officer locked us in in while I worked on a client, and unlocked the door when I was finished. When I first started my new job, I had just a few clients because the inmate population was mostly Black American women, most of who balked at a white girl cutting their hair, but I quickly proved that my skills were finely tuned. Most of the women were amazed that I could do a great job with their hair. Soon word traveled and I was busier than ever.

Meanwhile, my daughter had given birth to a beautiful baby boy named Karl Jay, whom I would not have the privilege of seeing until he was three months old. My great friend Sophia was the nucleus of my seeing my daughter and grandson. Sophia came to visit me weekly at the prison. Whenever she could arrange for Marie and Karl to accompany her, it was a real treat and surprise for me. Marie was living with her baby's father' stepmother and didn't get to speak with me very often, so we communicated through letters. It broke my heart that I had missed the birth of my grandchild and made me think of all the other life events I would miss, in the eight years of my confinement.

In many ways, however, ironically enough, Marie and I were closer than we ever had been. She explained to me that the reason why she became pregnant at age fifteen was because, as an adolescent, she had felt that she had lost everyone she loved in the world, and felt that having a baby would bring her comfort of the loved ones she had lost. Inadvertently, my situation had caused Marie to live a complete tragedy, stripping her of the life she had always known and leaving her parentless. The guilt that I felt was immeasurable. My heart ached when I thought of the inner turmoil my child had lived through, not to mention the difficulty of surviving in all alone because, although throughout the years, so many wonderful individuals had come to my aid, during my imprisonment, my family had showed a slight indifference and resentment toward Marie because it had been she who had secretly contacted Sean, her biological father.

But I understood. Marie was a curious child who was hurting from the absence of a father. Her desire to fit into a bigger picture in life had overshadowed her common sense. Her intention in contacting Sean was a harmless scream to be part of a family again, along with a lack of understanding of the real and immediate danger he posed.

As for my family, their only excuse—and it was, I suppose, a genuine one-was that she had brought him back into my life. As a result, during all the years I was imprisoned, Marie was left to fend for herself and her son. I can't fathom how I would have internalized the situation had I been she. But the fact was that Marie was the true victim in every sense of the word, although this was never recognized by anyone, not the State of Connecticut, not the family of her biological father, along with my family members as well. Not one of those individuals reached out to her to aid her during her traumatic transition. My mother and my stepfather were the only family members on either side that had stepped in on her behalf, and unfortunately, my mother's terminal illness had interrupted her ability to continue that loving care.

My mother's health was becoming increasingly poor. Her cancer had taken a toll on her ability to visit very often. I did speak with her on the phone in between the chemo treatments, and in that way, kept track of the effect it had on her physical state. Some days she could carry on a conversation and other days my stepfather would inform me that she was too ill to speak to anyone. As a result, my phone calls became less frequent and I resorted to letters and rare visits instead.

The unfortunate circumstances surrounding both my mother and my daughter fueled me to reach out for relief, from the imposed years of my set confinement, and slowly I began to pave a road for myself. I made it my business to be knowledgeable of the requirements for betterment during my stay there, researching the prison's inner-institutional programs that were available. I decided to become involved in any program provided that would show a productive prison record and started off signing up for various classes that were offered. In the facility everything was accomplished through sign-up sheets. Following a set deadline, the institution would hold classification meetings with the education staff and select inmates, per the classroom limitation. My first class was beginner's Spanish. I thought that, if nothing else, this would help me to communicate with the Latino population. The class was interesting but not helpful since all of the Spanish-speaking inmates used slang or "Spanglish", which is a made up combination of Spanish and English.

There was so much in the way of self-improvement at my command. I attended Al Anon each week. I participated in a literary course which trained inmates to teach other inmates how to read and write basic English. I took a homemaking class that included cooking, sewing and cleaning. This class was equal to a seventh grade upper elementary class. Most of the classes were geared toward the general population and the level of education for the majority of the prisoners, many of whom needed to work on their GED certification. My participation in the anger management class would, I knew, be important, because I had been sentenced for a violent crime, and when I noticed a paralegal course, I jumped at the opportunity to take a class that would actually stimulate my brain.

This class was interesting and informative, the only course that actually engaged my mind and challenged my intelligence. I was so interested in the laws and fact finding that, having researched outside correspondence colleges for para-legal studies, I found a reasonably priced course offered by a correspondence college, and was granted permission to participate in the outside course, as long as the payment for such a program was made by someone other than myself. My family paid for the para-legal class and I was on my way to receiving a diploma from a real academic institution.

Finally, I felt like I was achieving something positive, while incarcerated. I knew it would keep me focused and productive.

Later, during my stay in the maximum-security unit, a course called The A-M-E-R-I-C-A-N was offered, a course that was designed and instituted by a former football player named John White. However, this offering which had seemed so promising was a great disappointment since the entire program was designed to focus on drug addiction. The daily exercises seemed to be for individuals that had never functioned as productive adults, people who had never held a real job, or had lived a normal life, according to the society's standards, cult-like in its curriculum. Months later, I discovered that the founder of the program, a Mr. John White, had been arrested for abusing his wife and assaulting her. The very man who designed a program that was the rage in every prison in the State of Connecticut was himself an abuser. It came as no surprise when, after a while, the program faded out of existence completely.

After that terrible reality of the inner-workings of the prison system, I decided to research programs that were geared toward battered women, only to find that none were offered even though a large of number of women prisoners had suffered some abuse in their lives and that it was often the underlying cause for their being in prison. They had either been involved in crimes, as a sidekick for their abusive men, or prostituted for them. Others took the blame for drug charges their men had committed in the name of love, or what they perceived as love. A multitude of women had no idea that their lives had been filled with abuse.

And yet, despite all this, the prison did not offer group counseling or any type of program for abused women. It was hard to believe that the only State Prison Facility for women did not have a program to address the number one basis of women's issues. Instead, all of the programs that were offered addressed these inmates' lack of education and their drug addiction. Even the psychological counseling was only offered to inmates who were taking prescription drugs. As a result, I took out my word processor, and began writing letters to the institution's administration asking for answers to this obvious oversight. I wrote to the administrator's office, the psychological department and the social workers to no avail. The responses I received were nothing more than form letters acknowledging my request and a list of programs that were available programs that did not address any of the abusive issues toward women. I had gone full circle within the prison facility to no end.

Next, I decided to write a letter to the state's Division on Women in which I informed the director of the lack of programs for batter women in my facility. I further requested a program designed to counsel prison inmates who had suffered from abusive relationships. This time, I received a form letter informing me that the state of Connecticut did not have the funds in their budget for such a program and was further informed that, at such time that the state acquires such funds, they would consider instituting such a program. Again, I had come to a dead end, but I was determined not to give up.

Going to the legal library, I looked up the addresses for each and every battered woman's organization in the state of Connecticut and took note of one address for each of the eight counties, after which I sent out letters introducing myself and giving a short description of my own experiences and an update as to the status of the prison system's lack of programs, ending my letters with a request for help. Most of the few responses I received informed me that they were not funded for such a program until finally a battered women's organization in Montville informed me that they would contact the prison facility's administration and provide a volunteer to institute a program for women in the maximum-security unit. I was beyond thrilled with the news. It gave me a beacon of hope that one person's persistence could make a difference.

Within a few months, this agency sent out a volunteer to institute group counseling. The once-a-week meetings, which took place in Pierce Hall, began by attracting ten women. Ellen, a woman in her mid-sixties who conducted these meetings always wore some variation of the color purple which signified support for the survival of battered women.

Ellen's intentions were fine, but she tended to conduct classes as though she were a elementary school teacher, and used, over and over, the same sort of paperwork, most of which showed the wheel of abuse, something that all of us were all too familiar with. Bored, we came up with a project that would involve all of us at our own personal level, including posters, and in my case, a patchwork quilt which I offered to sew together after each woman had hand sewn a few squares depicting a symbol of their abuse.

The project took months to organize, since there had to be authorization for materials supplied. Each woman would sew the squares on their own and hand them in to me for the final construction. Each square was an applique of layered material decorated with different shapes and messages. The result, when all forty-four handmade squares were assembled, was not only therapeutic for all of us, but a work of art. The quilt, entitled "Forgotten Names" was beautiful when finished, it's border being cut outs of women standing hand-in-hand. The facility officials were so pleasantly surprised by the final project that the Warden decided to hang the quilt permanently in the administration building's boardroom. Years later the quilt project was elevated in status by being shown during a tour of the governor's office.

This experience taught me a good deal, including the fact that women who had crossed the line deemed by society as acceptable in order to defend themselves against an abusers were viewed as monsters, no doubt because the public has been so accustomed to hearing the numerous deaths of battered women at the hands of their abusers, not the contrary. People like Ellen should have publicized the fact that these so-called murderers, had chosen to take a life rather than to lose their own.

Ellen's intentions were good, but she missed the opportunity to make her peers aware of just how an abused woman can be pushed to the point of committing murder, contenting herself, as far as I could tell, with explaining that she was not afraid of us. I thought of how sad it was that some people start out doing good work, and then somehow let their ego become involved. I believed that Ellen was proud to be doing the work with us for more reasons other than just helping the poor women who had crossed the line. I really believe that she was completely unaware of her ego-based motives. Her colleagues viewed her, as a martyr or hero. My opinion at the time was that it was hard for Ellen to pass up the recognition. It showed me that she was not professionally equipped to deal with us, and that; as a consequence, she went through our program therapy blindly. And so, although some good had come out of the program she had conducted, thanks in good part to inmate' efforts, I decided to enter a plea for clemency to the governor's office, and asked her to write a letter of support on my behalf, only to have my hopes crushed when she explained that there was no possibility of that happening.

Later, although heartbroken, I was fueled by her negativity. I set my mind on my goal and the core reasons for my request which was that my daughter desperately needed me and my mother, who was would not live for much longer, required my care. These were the factors that drove me to realize my dreams, not those of a stranger who did not understand me. Shortly thereafter, another woman in the group announced that she intended to go back to court with a motion to reconsider her thirty year sentence. Ellen couldn't do enough to help this particular prisoner. At first I was hurt, but then I realized that Ellen fed off of the weak and helpless, unlike someone such as me who was focused and headstrong, and as a consequence, determined to stay on my designed path.

During the days, weeks and months that passed, I kept occupied with a number of projects, including a collection of poetry, many of which I shared with our group and which I submitted for copy write to the United States Library of Congress. Creative writing really relieved some of my emotions. I searched for every therapeutic outlet I could find, and often found it in my wing mates, many of whom were among the most interesting individuals I had ever encountered. One of these was Lizzy, a seventy something woman serving a repeat sentence of extortion, having posed as Jacqueline Kennedy Onassis on the Internet, and another named Bonnie who had been sentenced to a thirty-year mandatory term for killing her boyfriend and her son with a barbeque skewer. And since Bonnie was so quiet and self-contained, it came as a shock when an officer found a journal in which she had targeted those of us, including me who she referred to as, "Margo, the beauty queen," as being on her "hit list."

And then there was Merial, who suffered from diabetes and was serving a ten-year sentence for shooting her mentally abusive husband at a family picnic, an event which she could not remember, no doubt because she was in the midst of a diabetic attack, of the sort that I had occasion to witness over the years since regulating the injection of Insulin was not a prison priority or specialty.

During my stay at this prison facility, I picked up many different ways to make my cell more a home. For example, I learned that I could heat up my clothing iron until hot, take a cold cheese sandwich inside a brown paper bag, press it on the hot iron and have a grilled cheese sandwich in minutes. My hot pot could do wondrous things, too, brewing boiling hot water in a few no time at all. With great care, and the right spices, that hot pot could heat a can of chicken, and some plain rice. Hot apples drizzled with sugar weren't bad either. As for my personal grooming, there was no such thing as going to a dentist to have a routine tooth cleaning since teeth were either filled or pulled. So I figured out that if I cleaned my tweezers real well, I could use them to scrape the tarter off my teeth. As far as pedicures or podiatry care was concerned, I discovered that, by taking my leg-shaving razor to my heels and toes, I could remove the calluses easily. I even showed more creativity when I mixed sugar or salt together with body lotion, and exfoliated my dry skin, a combination that also worked well for facial treatments. There was a host of ingenious ideas that people came up in prison to make it seem as though they were living in the ordinary world.

Other factors combined to make my life more manageable. Complete strangers that had learned about my case in the media extended their support to me through thoughtful cards, letters and books, and once even flowers. And there was the media sources which I discovered could help as well as harm. For example, a woman named Julie Portman who worked for a New York newspaper followed my case closely, and had written a sympathetic article when I had first been arrested. My attorneys remained in contact with her and I felt comfortable and confident enough to grant her a personal interview. I really believed that she would get the truth out in the local public. She came to the prison and interviewed me on two occasions, once when I first arrived and again when I decided to file for clemency to the governor's office. I was pleasantly surprised that her written articles were both so honest and empathic that remained hopeful that, with more awareness there would come more understanding and less judgment in my case and that of other women.

Another writer named Ellen Mirth, worked for my hometown news station, and wrote articles for *Darien's Post News*. She inquired about interviewing me for a human-interest story, one that would examine how my imprisonment had affected my daughter and other members of my family. It was a really different spin on the sad predicament everyone was living through at the time. Ellen was an extremely caring individual who I felt "got it." She thought outside the immediate circumstances, and looked further into the ramifications on others involved in my life. As a consequence, I was happy to grant her permission to interview me, conducting our interview in the Madison Hall Maximum security kitchen. For over two hours we sat and talked candidly, following which she interviewed my daughter and wrote the most beautiful and poignant article to date. For many years after our encounter Ellen wrote to me, often urging me to have my story turned into a movie script, something for which, as I explained to her in a letter, I was not yet ready, although the suggestion brought me comfort and hope.

The article Ellen produced was a tremendous help for my daughter. Not only did people contact her, expressing desire to assist her economically, but also it brought her in touch with her adopted father, Scott, who had not been in contact with her for years.

Scott picked up some of the broken pieces of my daughter's sad life. Her stepped up and supported her as the adopted father he had vowed to be when she was three years old. He helped her get a car and go back to school, and with his assistance, she began to get back on her feet. And I was not excluded. When he brought Marie and Karl to visit me, I saw that he had become a mature, well-rounded adult. He thanked me for supporting him for so many years, and assured me that I deserved being helped now in my time of need. As time progressed, Scott and I communicated more frequently. He took the time to send me clothing, music and books. He wrote me letters and continued to bring my daughter and grandson to weekend visits, bringing with him a variety of delicious culinary delights. His reappearance in both our lives, as a mature, caring and successful man, willing and able to contribute and show his love and gratitude, came at a very emotional time, one in which Marie was breaking her inherited history of abuse, and my mother was dying.

Scott remained in my life for a many years, during which time, he himself benefited from the renewed relationship. But since there seemed to be no future for us, it came as no surprise that ultimately he met and married someone and moved forward with his life, keeping both Marie and I in his heart. In retrospect, I clearly viewed our reunion, as a life-saving raft that kept me afloat, at a time of great need.

TWENTY

Legal Office Prison Career

THAT FALL, I WAS CALLED to a classification meeting only to discover that, because of an opening in the legal office in Madison Hall, I was to be taken on as a paralegal to replace her. And since I would not only receive more prison work credits but also a higher salary, it was a win-win situation. I was excited to accept the challenge.

Although the law office was only the size of a medium broom closet, it was lined with book shelve, and capably run by Mr. Calvin, who also taught Electronics and computer repair, a nice older man who was so overworked with his various jobs that he welcomed my persistence when it came to requesting supplies.

An inmate named Wendy showed me the ins and outs of the legal office. She gave me form letters and motions to follow when I was called upon to submit these different documents for prisoners. She also introduced me to the procedures followed by the office in regard to research, as well as acquainting me with the different court reports that contained the legal cases of thousands of criminals so that I was quickly versed on all the updated information regarding the Connecticut statues controlling the institutional regulations and rules. This paperwork was an enormous part of my job, in that law office, and I was thankful that Wendy was able to give me sufficient training before she was transferred.

The hours spent in the para-legal office was composed of writing letters, motions and appeals to the different courts in the state of Connecticut on inmate security units prisoners. Many times I would interview women who had detainers for other crimes they had been charged with in different

Connecticut counties, women who were asking the court to accept the letter, as a document where the inmate choose to plead guilty to the pending charges, on the condition that the court ran the new sentence concurrent with their present sentence imposed. Otherwise, the prisoner would be forced to complete one sentence and then go on to serve another concurrent sentencing saved the state the financial burden of transporting the prisoner to the different counties, as well as, the cost of her additional confinement. Some of the woman requested that their criminal sentence be appealed to the federal courts on the basis of their having had ineffective assistance of counsel. This would involve researching federal case law, in support of their claim. I would type these multiple page appeals and forward them to the court for review. I also wrote motions to the state courts asking them to reconsider the sentence. Sometimes the court would show mercy and grant a reduced sentence. Often times these motions were denied immediately.

Once a week I would go into the reception unit of the prison, and interview the newly arrived inmates and address any legal issues they might have pending. The priority of my workload was determined by an appointment submitted by the individual prisoner. On rare occasions, I would be taken to the mental health unit, located in Clark Cottage, situated separately from the entire institution's regular housing units where I had many immigration matters to resolve for inmates that were considered illegal aliens.

My job also involved interviews of women who had been accused of institutional infractions, women I had to represent at a disciplinary hearing. Some of them had been accused of an infraction that was to take them to the lock-down unit, while they awaited a hearing. Other prisoners, less seriously accused, had blue sheet charges pending against them.

All such inmates, however, were entitled to representation from an inmate para-legal. In the prison disciplinary system, unlike the general judicial system, an inmate was guilty until proven innocent. I would read over the blue sheet, interview them, and their witnesses, check to see that all of their due process rights were honored, and then prepare their defense. If they were present, I would speak for them at the disciplinary hearing, and I also wrote disciplinary appeals for the punishment instituted. First,

I had to interview each and every inmate who was transferred to the segregated lock unit after undergoing the indignity of a full body search.

I must confess that working in the law office put me in a much better position to interact with the inmates. I was, naturally, given an entire new level of respect, in the eyes of the other prisoners, particularly since, in this environment, the amount of respect you were due was directly related to the influence you could wield, and now I was able to succeed in applying my legal knowledge to aid in my own comforts and safety, having accidentally discovered an entire new realm of living free from harassment, especially after winning my first big assault case for an inmate accused of stabbing another prisoner. Reading over the paperwork, I noticed that the times of the statements conflicted with other written statements by the officer and that the witness's statements also supported my argument of innocence. Consequently, as a result of the inmates due rights having been violated, the charges were dismissed and I was labeled as someone who could successfully defend prisoner rights, and was referred to as "Miss" as though I, too, were not an inmate.

Working in the paralegal office also gave me the sort of inside information that I could use in my own defense, and as a result, I began to review all of the mitigating circumstances that would show the court that my sentence was a hardship on my terminally ill mother, as well as my child who was in her own abusive relationship. When I finally submitted the motion to the court, I did so with the unrealistic expectation that the documents I produced would be sufficient to convince a judge that my sentence should be reduced. Little did I know that this would be the beginning of a long and tedious battle that would continue until my final release from imprisonment.

However, I was no longer naïve enough not to hedge my bets and in doing I discovered that, on rare occasions, the governor of the state of Connecticut could grant mercy toward prisoners through a Clemency Petition. I contacted my former attorneys and requested all of my documentation from my sentencing, along with any other pertinent information that would aid me in writing my petition, after receipt of which, I wrote a personal letters to all of the battered women's groups requesting support of my request for clemency. I sent letters to each and every individual that I had ever known, asking them for letters to support my request as well. The clemency process was an extremely long, drawn out ordeal, unlike relief requested from the court system. I spend many painstaking hours typing the brief that I attached to my request. And then, having collected every mitigating factor, I held my breath, and mailed the thick package off to the governor's office.

Shortly after mailing my petition for clemency relief, my mother's health took a turn for the worst. The doctors at the hospital had deemed my mother's cancer fatal and basically told her there was nothing more they could do for her medically, and suggested that hospice be contacted since she had been in and out of the hospital for some time. Her heart was weak and when the doctors found that the chemotherapy drugs were too much for her heart to handle, they stopped them and let her disease takes its course. But because she was on blood thinners to prevent further strokes and the medication was not regulated properly, her leg pooled with blood and peritonitis set in, which meant a return to the hospital. Now I had to make a horrible decision, to choose between my mother's funeral service, or a bedside death visit.

In the state of Connecticut, the laws governing inmates could be taken to dying family member's funeral or make a bedside visit if the family member was fatally ill. The funeral for my mother was going to take place in the Bronx where she was born and raised, so I would not have been permitted to attend, due to the it being held out the state where I was imprisoned. All of this left me with no choose but to settle for a bedside visit with my mother.

When, one day, an officer came to my cell and told me to get dressed in a state-issued uniform and not to use the phone or leave my room, until she came back to get me, I had no idea what was happening to me. It wasn't unusual for an inmate to be moved anywhere at any time as part of the prison's system control method which was based on the premise that prisoners should always be kept in the dark. When the officer returned to my room, and told me I was going out of the facility for a bedside visit and that I was to report to the medical facility immediately, I knew that this must concern my mother, and my heart began to pound so hard that I felt dizzy.

The last time I had seen my mom had been on the occasion when my sister Joan had brought her up to the prison to see me, and now I remembered all too vividly, the shock I had experienced when I had seen her waiting at the steel table for my arrival. She had lost about sixty pounds, along with her beautiful mane of auburn colored hair, her head now covered with a poorly styled synthetic wig. She looked like she had aged at least twenty years in just a few months.

Now, about to see her once again, I was off to the medical building to begin the barbaric ritual of being strip searched, before leaving the institution, after which I was rushed off to a holding cell to await the transportation officers where I met two correctional officers, who cuffed my wrists and shackled my feet, the handcuffs being attached to a wide brown leather belt, which they tightened around my torso. The problem was that my waistline was too small for the belt to fit properly. Officer Conti made a joke about how little I was and for me not to slip the handcuffs, but I didn't get his humor. Officer Jones had to fasten the leather belt around me looping the straps twice around my body, instead of the usual once and I was loaded into the back of the van and was on my way, but not before drawing up to what looked like a bank teller's building where one of the officers slipped my paperwork and identification into a drawer, only to retrieve my documents along with two firearms.

It was explained that this was happening because I was "hot," which meant that my criminal case was well known via the media, making me a flight risk. I assured him that I was not "hot" in that capacity, and that I certainly wasn't an escape risk, especially with two firearms pointing at me. All I wanted to do is see my dying mother. He laughed and told me not to worry about any labels attached to me, because he was confident that I wasn't going to try and get away.

The drive to the hospital took about an hour. Odel's eatery remained standing on Route 1, and other buildings were equally so familiar that I felt a sense of great loss. All of the memories I had of this town stammered through my brain, but only a traffic light away from the hospital, I tried to calm myself. I was afraid to see my mother helplessly stricken in a hospital bed, especially knowing that this would be the last time I would see her. I was overcome by emotion, but I held back the wellspring of tears, for fear that the officers would think I was unstable. One of the lessons I'd learned as a prisoner was that, if I displayed any type of extreme emotions, it would be interpreted as cause for alarm. The tears on my cheeks dried naturally because with the belted handcuffs I was unable to reach my face to wipe them.

When we arrived at my mother's hospital room, after attracting a certain amount of attention in the lobby thanks to my shackles, I found her to be a shell of her former self. Tears rolling down my cheeks, I reached out to touch her hand and saw her smile at me as she opened her eyes. She was truly happy to see me even though I was wearing handcuffs.

My mother was on morphine to help her deal with the tremendous pain she was suffering, but the medication made her slip in and out of consciousness, literally fading away in mid-sentence. At other times during our visit, my mother would stop talking and wince in pain. It was gut-wrenching for me. I desperately wanted to reach out and take away her illness. Instead, we talked and talked about everything that meant so much to both of us, my daughter and stepfather and my younger sister everything, but her death. The only time we referred to her dying was right before I was leaving when she whispered that she was tired of fighting the pain, tired of her body shrinking away to nothing, tired of being tired.

Despite the fact that even the thought of losing her was painful beyond endurance, I told her that it was all right to let go, even though, like a child, I wanted to cry out, "Don't leave me! I can't bear to let you go!" It was an epic turning moment in my life, one that I could never erase from my mind or heart. My loss became a sadness that consumed me. As usual, she was more concerned about my well being than her own. She was such a beautiful person, kind and full of pride that she didn't deserve to suffer that way. It was so unfair and unwarranted. If given the choice, I would have gladly taken her place. Unfortunately, we weren't afforded that option.

My mother, even on her deathbed, was still the tower of strength I had always known her to be although I'm sure it took all the strength she could muster up to put on this façade for my benefit. She told me to never quit fighting and to remain strong always. My heart melted, as I kissed her cheek for what I knew was the last time and whispered, "I love you," as the officers escorted me out of the room.

TWENTY-ONE

Psychological Ordeal Fuels Renewal

WITH THE NEWS OF MY mother's death, I fell into a deep depression. It was the first time in my confinement that I had felt such emptiness, so emotionally crippled. After lock down every evening, I found myself silently crying a river of tears. For weeks I walked about the facility in a state of numbness. Whenever an inmate's loved one passes away, the institution automatically puts that inmate on close watch since death of a family member causes a red flag alert for the administration which assumes the prisoner will somehow act out violently in some way, or attempt an escape.

In theory, it seemed to make sense to me, but living like that kept me from the human process of mourning the loss of my loved one. I never was afforded the chance to grieve the loss of my mother; in the way I would have naturally done had I not been subjected to scrutiny. Instead I had to hide the tears and the sinking feeling of depression. I put on my mask, just as I had to hide the abuse I had suffered at the hands of Sean. It wasn't really that different. My heart was broken. For the first time, I absolutely connected with the feelings that my own daughter must have held inside of her when she found herself parentless forever, too soon, too abruptly. The hopelessness of never seeing my mother again enveloped my being. Many days during count time, when it was quiet and safe, I would talk to her. I found myself begging her to show me a sign that she was with me. I questioned my belief in God. I was in a hole, being sucked into the dark pool of despair from which I was unexpectedly rescued by the news that a man from Hartford Connecticut was coming to conduct an in-depth psychological evaluation. The officer didn't have any further information for me.

I practically ran back to my cell to get ready because it was really happening. My clemency petition was finally going forward. I could have screamed with delight. But then I considered the reality of the situation and faced the fact that this would mean an in-depth evaluation of the sort I had not been forced to endure for a long time.

Mr. McQuire, who had been sent by the governor's office to conduct an in-depth psychological evaluation to accompany my clemency petition, immediately put me at ease by asking about my earliest childhood, going on to ask me to describe my relationship with Sean in great detail. And so it was that, with no reservations, I shared every memory of the events of that time in my life in vivid detail. I desperately wanted this man to understand what I experienced so that he would fully comprehend why my life's path arrived at the present road. He seemed professional and empathic throughout the evaluation. At times, when I stopped because I was overpowered by emotion, Mr. McQuire waited patiently for me to compose myself before he continued.

Gently, he led me through the events that lead to my criminal action. It was difficult to relive and retell all this to a complete stranger, especially when I knew he was analyzing every word that came out of my mouth, which caused me a good deal of anxiety. I wanted him to know that I was a good person, and tried desperately to make him aware that I was a normal loving law-abiding citizen that had been forced into a horrible situation, which had resulted in my frantic attempt to save my life. Being forced to remember it all in such detail exhausted me so emotionally that I believed my skull was going to explode.

However, Mr. McQuire was not yet finished with my evaluation. Next I was given a battery of psychological tests which began with a written exam to evaluate my present mental status, after which I took a Rorschach test in which I was asked to look at the inkblot and say whatever came to my mind, a process that made me feel as though I were on a train going full speed toward a brick wall. Mr. McQuire topped this session off by asking me to draw a picture of Sean and although I was no Michelangelo, I did my best.

Mr. McQuire picked up the drawing from the desk and said, "We are finished here for now. If I have further questions I will return to see you. But for now I must analyze what I have learned and write my report". He concluded by reminding me that clemency was a very lengthy process and that I shouldn't expect an answer for a long time to come.

I returned to my cell completely devoid of all energy. After having been through five hours of testing and talking, my head aching, my body so limp from pure fatigue that I collapsed on my bed. I didn't know how to feel about the evaluation. I couldn't tell if I had presented myself well, although I knew that I had tried my very best to convey to this man the human being behind the inmate number.

It was a week later when Mr. McQuire returned to follow up with a few more questions, and this time the atmosphere was completely different, imbued as it was with a sense of urgency which was increased when he asked me straight out whether or not I had shot Sean. Seeing that Mr. McQuire seemed to be increasingly annoyed by my answers, I looked straight at him and said, "I have nothing to hide or nothing to gain from lying to you or anyone else. If I had shot Sean I would definitely tell you so, but I didn't shoot him and that is the truth of the matter".

Mr. McQuire then tried to present a scenario in which anyone might think I would lie about being the shooter. He went on to say that I might be protecting my daughter by lying. I immediately told him that, if I had been the shooter, my daughter would understand and I wouldn't hide it from her or anyone else. I also added that had I simply claimed to have shot Sean; I would have been given a shorter sentence and a more rapid resolution to my case. Because I didn't shoot him, my entire case was more complicated and the results were worse. I felt as though the abuse that drove me to commit my criminal offense was lost in the quest for the shooter. I shared with Mr. McQuire that, in my opinion, I was punished more severely for not having committed the crime. I said that, although it made more sense that I would have been the person who shot Sean, it was absolutely not the case. I said, "However I take full responsibility for Sean's death today as I did the day I was sentenced."

When I had finished, I saw Mr. McQuire's pupils constricted to the size of a pinhead. I could literally feel his frustration and anger. "Well there is no sense in beating a dead horse any further"! he said and then apologized for his outburst. When he left the room, he didn't look back. This was not a good moment. Doom enveloped me when I walked out of the classroom.

It was at this point that I made a conscience decision to gather up as much support as possible to counter balance Mr. McQuire's personal opinion of the identity of Sean's actual shooter. I could not change the truth, and I had already been browbeaten enough, for not being guilty. Unfortunately, Mindy was never going to own up to her part in this crime, so I had to make the best of the never ending, lingering question which I knew I must prepare myself for people to ask me for the rest of my life.

I decided to contact my oldest sister Joan and ask her to start a petition to be signed by people in the communities in which I had lived to plea for clemency with the result that, months later, she had collected over one thousand signatures on my behalf. I forwarded the petition to the governor's office to add to my file. And whenever I received letters of support from former clients and friends, I sent them out to be added to them. I also contacted all of the battered women's groups I knew of, requesting their aid. The Coalition for the Defense of Battered Women's director Sally Osterman was instrumental in collecting support for me. Unfortunately, her agency was located in New York City, and had little influence on Connecticut's office of the governor.

Still, I refused to give up my networking and reaching out to the community for help. Contacting my attorney's office, I shared with them my plan for public support. Julie Warren, one of my lawyers, thought it was a great idea to gather up as much support as possible while my clemency petition was still pending, and contacted Julie Portland, who had done an earlier interview after my sentencing and now agreed to assist.

The interview took place in the same office in the maximum-security building and I found Julie very friendly and supportive of my entire situation. I updated her on all the different programs I had involved myself with since my arrival, along with my current position in the legal office. I shared the tragedy of losing my mother while incarcerated and the hardship of having my daughter so alone and estranged during my confinement with the result that Julie produced the nicest article in support of my request for clemency. I was so grateful that she took a personal interest in my life-altering situation. Following our interview, Julie and my attorneys appeared on a local talk show to speak about my plight. Julie was sweet enough to put her reputation on the line to support my request. She also labeled my crime as an act of desperation to save my life.

During a religious meeting, I spoke with a Rabbi Jacob who ran a Jewish temple located in Norwich, a mild-mannered kindly man who was gracious enough, to take time out of his busy schedule to visit with prisoners. Rabbi Jacob came to the prison to give spiritual counseling on a weekly basis even though I was one of only two inmates in the entire institution that practiced the Jewish religion and it was he who, miraculously enough, happened to be on the board of the Women's Abuse Center for the state and was, as a consequence, in close contact with its director, told me that he would speak to her on my behalf. I firmly believed that this connection was a divine intervention.

I was finally moved to minimum security. The big moment in my incarceration had arrived. It was the early spring of 1998 when I was move to the minimum-security grounds compound, leaving my years of maximum security confinement behind me. Having fulfilled half of my sentence, at last I could see light at the end of the tunnel. I packed all of my belongings into three large boxes, discovering as I did so, that the comforts of my own room had resulted in my having gathered more things than I had realized. As my van pulled away from the grounds I once thought I would never leave, I was as wide eyed as a child.

The first building we passed was, as I later learned, Roosevelt Cottage and beyond it a brick building which the driver told me was the Education Building, beyond which was Arthur Cottage where those prisoners in drug rehabilitation programs were housed.

At the top of a steep hill, beyond the administration building, stood a very old chapel, and beyond that Brook Cottage, my new home. But it was not the building that struck me so forcefully; it was the freedom reflected in the rural surroundings and the well-kept lawns, not to mention the fact that there were no correctional officers to be seen, but only women prisoners strolling about, talking to one another as though they were living in the outside world which I had nearly forgotten.

I snapped back into reality when I heard my unit officer's voice. She was a tall black woman, who towered over most of the women that stood near me as she directed us to come inside with our boxes. Beyond the officer's desk area was a television room and on the opposite side a large open kitchen. It all looked so institutional that my heart sank when I realized that, after having my own private cell for three years, I was now going to be assigned to a dorm area, but I told myself that I had to see the positive in the situation. Women in the minimum-security compound moved up faster than those in the maximum-security units. Unlike max where most of the inmates were serving life sentences or a long term sentence with mandatory minimum fulfillments, most of the women living out on grounds, were ready to go home on parole or to a half-way house which meant, I discovered, that the bed rotation would move quicker. I was thrilled to hear that fact. I told myself that I was a stronger and wiser person and I would survive just fine.

My job assignment was that of a para-professional teacher's assistant for the electronics/computer diagnostics class which was taught by the same Mr. Calvin who had been my boss when I worked in the para-legal office in the maximum unit, and who was now instrumental in seeing that I received the first available full para-legal assignment. And so it was that my new life began, one I embraced eagerly, certain that this time I could become the woman I had always wanted to be.

One of the first rules I leaned was to always keep moving. Standing around in the hallways was considered a loitering violation, just as it was outside where it was imperative that you kept to the walkway. There was a sign-up sheet for everything including telephone usage, laundry facilities, day and evening movements with the exception of work movement. The officer called out a five-minute warning, before each movement was about to occur. If you signed up for a movement that meant your attendance was mandatory.

Everything operated on a schedule, including the opening of refrigerators at set times in the morning, afternoon and evening when the officer would unlock the refrigerator and allow the women to take out their personal cooked food. Anytime during the day we could go into the kitchen and use the microwave and the tables and chairs. Most of the time, the prisoners were in the kitchen not eating but playing card games.

All and all, it was a really busy place to live. There was always something happening.

A short while after being transferred to the grounds unit, the medical staff came around to do the yearly tuberculosis testing on each inmate with the result that, the very next day, I was called to the medical building. Apparently, I had been exposed to tuberculosis when interviewing inmates in the reception unit in maximum security. I had to have an x-ray to see if there was damage to my lungs, and also had to take medication every day for a period of six months.

The medication line was outside Arthur Cottage. All of the inmates would line up and wait their turn to go to the nurses' window. After receiving the medication, it was customary to open your mouth and show the officer you had swallowed the drug. This was the most miserable process. In rain, snow sleet or sun, we stood in line outside like cattle waiting for slaughter. Usually, I never took any medication for the simple reason the process was too barbaric to bother. If I was sick, I let my body repair itself. I could buy my own allergy medication at the commissary, so if I felt a cold coming on, I took my own remedy.

However, my tuberculosis exposures lead to a mandatory medication prescription. One evening while waiting in line, an inmate that stood behind me tapped me on the shoulder, and began telling me that she knew me. I didn't recognize her and said she must have mistaken me for someone else, but she insisted that she did know me and then she told me that she had been at the Amtrak train line the night Sean beat me with a club. When I ask her if she ever thought of calling the police for help, she shook her head and said that she was sorry for not calling, adding, "I just minded my own business. I didn't want any trouble." It gave me chills up my spine that a witness had stood inches away from me being beaten and dragged across a public parking lot, and had not cared enough to call for help! It was a strange feeling to know that if this one woman had taken a different course of action and reported Sean's behavior, I might not be where I was right now.

The education building was enormous, accommodating, as it did, several different classrooms, a gymnasium, a beauty school, the law office and a parole hearing room. When I first walked into the building, there was an enclosed desk area, which was for the correctional officer while another walked the hallways of the building. Every morning, after showing the desk officer my identification badge, I reported to work. My job, which was to help the students with their studies and computer repair equipment, was hectic at first but it became second nature as the days rolled forward. Mr. Calvin was a slender man with an appealing sense of humor. He told hundreds of jokes a week. The man was really a caring individual who never passed judgment on the inmates with whom he worked. Actually, he was rather fond of them. He had so many responsibilities at that facility that at times, he was a bit overwhelmed, a man with many hats so to speak. He was in charge of the law offices for both complexes, taught electronics/ computer repair class and was involved with the institution's education assembly. Mr. Calvin was about five years away from retirement and counting down the days.

I was introduced to Mr. Calvin's other para-professional, an overweight girl named Dana Little who wore her hair styled like that of an eighties rock star. It was a very dated look, but she seemed to have embraced it. Despite the girlish attire she favored, she seemed somehow masculine and I was not surprised when, later, I met her partner, Megan, another para-legal. Dana and Megan showed me the ins and outs of the education building and all that went with it. It was nice to have people who didn't have a motive to aid me in my transition.

I was excited about the new visiting procedures which took place in the gymnasium. During a visit, my family, friends and I were able to sit in plastic chairs facing each other, so close that our knees were actually touching. The only negative aspect of a visit was when they ended. Prisoner's loved ones had to stand on one side of the gym and the inmates on the opposite side so that the officers could count the visitors and then the inmates. Because we were able to wear street clothes, the officers were very careful with the count in order to make sure that none of the inmates were walking out of the gym to freedom. Once families were escorted through the door, the officers would make us line up and wait to be stripped searched.

My daughter and grandson would often visit with my friend Sophia. My daughter was doing well in those days. Her father, Scott, bought her a new car and was paying for her education at the local community college. Shortly after my move to minimum security, she landed a full time job as a manager of a shoe store in Darien, and was now well on her way to becoming a stable, mature adult. I was so proud of her strength and perseverance. In my mind, as long as Marie was doing well, I could live each day with a tremendous inner peace.

So many people helped me now, including talented dedicated people like Cherrie who had been sentenced to a term of thirty years for drug distribution and manufacturing. Unlike most incarcerated drug dealers or drug addicts, she was well versed in the law as well as in life, a very well rounded person all business and serious when it came to legal matters. I learned quite a lot from her to prepare myself for the big fight against the system, and as a result of my association with her and those like her, I also began attending weekly meeting of the institute's chapter of AA, NA and Al Anon, as well as anything that would keep me busy and focused. My days flew by and before I knew it, I had been out on grounds for almost a year.

During that year my Rabbi had contacted the director of the Women's Abuse Center in Norwich Connecticut, a woman named Naomi Canter, who was very interested in my life experience and requested the legal documentation on my criminal case. I immediately contacted my former attorney, Julie Warren, and asked if she would be kind enough to send Naomi my court documents. Julie had always kept in touch with me, having been so sincere and kind all throughout my incarceration, and now she contacted Naomi and shared my legal history, and also communicated her opinion of my character, as well. Within a few weeks Naomi contacted the institution and requested a meeting with me, along with the women's center's attorney, transitional housing liaison, and a board member. I was called up to the Administration building the following week, for a two hour private meeting with these wonderful people.

Naomi was beyond kind and understanding. I explained that I needed support for my clemency petition by way of their agency affording me placement for one year in the transitional housing program, and then met the attorney from the agency and the woman who was in charge of the extended housing. The last to speak was a very attractive and stately older woman named Babs McCarthy, a former legislator who was the first woman in the state to help pass the domestic violence laws.

As soon as Babs became chairmen of the board of directors for the Women's Abuse Center, I felt charged up because of all of the empathy and support that was extended to me. I had been imprisoned for over four years, and during that time, some of my fire, my self-confidence, self-esteem and spirit had been smothered. During the two hours that followed, we discussed my life experience and my hopes for the future. All of the individuals in the room had already read and studied my case file. The mechanics of my abusive past relationship were of no surprise to them. They understood, they empathized, validated and supported me.

The amazing thing was that these were respectable people who were well versed in the cycle of abusive backgrounds and they support me. I was touched and so hopeful that someone believed in me and wanted to help. I know that, during my sentencing, many people supported me, but they were people I had known all my life. These people were complete strangers and yet they were extending the same provisions as if I had known them my entire life. At the conclusion of our meeting, there wasn't a dry eye in the room, particularly after Bab's told me that she wanted me to know that, when she had read my story, she had been overcome with sorrow for the injustices that had been thrown in my path. Babs further stated, she would do everything in her power to get me out of that place. Hearing her words, I began to cry and before long everyone in the room was crying. I began with a request for support for clemency and ended up with a sheer miracle. Naomi and Babs would be my voice in society. I was convinced that each of them had real angel wings.

I left the Administration Building feeling grateful and blessed, practically skipping back to Brook Cottage. Now I knew what path I must peruse. Whenever I could, I wrote to influential people out in society for support of my petition for clemency. I even contacted murdered Nicole Brown Simpson's family for support. They answered with a kind letter supporting my fight for freedom. The Abuse Center prepared the most wonderful post release plan to be included in my petition to the governor and didn't stop there. Naomi started a signature petition for my clemency. I was amazed at the support they gathered, on my behalf. Babs told me that she and my Rabbi were having a meeting with a local United States senator, Leon Land, on my behalf. The meeting was to request support from him for my release by the governor, John L. Row, a resident of New

London County Connecticut which, miraculously was where the Abuse Center was located, I was more hopeful than I could ever have dreamed of being. My networking was beginning to bear fruit. Along the way I kept busy and focused on my days of freedom to come. I believed in a higher hand in my quest for release.

In March 1999, I was re-classified to the ground's para-legal office. It was a seven-day a week work credit, and I would gain more time served off my total sentence. For each month I held that job, I gained three days extra as days served. The office was amazingly large, equipped with computers and big wooden desks. We had our own desk and a legal secretary to do all the filing and legal copies for the court. Since legal work was protected and private, the officers did not bother us there, and we were shown respect by the prison population and the officers as well.

The woman who befriended me there had the quickest fingers that I've ever seen move on a computer keyboard. I was amazed by her skill and knowledge of that legal office. I soaked up all of the information Megan shared with me because, since she was about six months from ending her criminal sentence, I would soon be taking over her office.

In the interim, I noticed that there were a large number of parole denials coming into the legal office on appeal, most of them because of the lack of one-on-one counseling unless the inmate was on some type of medication, which posed a question. How could they demand one-on-one counseling when it was not available in our institution? But when I wrote to the administration about the matter, I was told at first that there was no extra money in the facility's budget for one-on-one counseling. But thanks to the efforts of Naomi on my behalf a councilor was found, one who not only worked with women individually, but also extended services to the institution for abuse awareness and therapy. She held assemblies and planned projects for the women to participate in. Not only did Naomi provide information to the abused women, but she also educated the women that were abusers themselves. It was a monumental leap in the facility's programs, one which led to a clothesline project, in which all of the inmates designed tee shirts that were exhibited on clotheslines in Norwich, an event that connected us to the outside world.

Naomi also arranged for a play called *The Purple Dress* to be performed at our institution. It was about a battered girl who was murdered by her abusive boyfriend during a prom dance, a fact that does not become apparent until well into the middle of the performance. This was still another example of Naomi's bringing the attention of the public to the problem of battered women.

Life in the prison was always exciting for one reason or another, particularly since, whenever the inmates of the men's prison violated a rule, we were all penalized, if not by a lock down by more aggressive responses such as the metal slats being removed from the head and footboards of our beds because one of the male inmates had succeeded in making a knife out of one of them.

Other events were the notorious fire drills. I remember being rushed from my room, fire alarms screaming in my ears, and finding out it was all a false alarm, during which, standing in silence in a perfectly straight line with our inmate identification card in our hand, we would have to submit to our identification being checked while officers in combat gear, looking as though they were prepared for a public riot, went through our belongings as though we were hiding explosives.

The year of 1999 was an unsettling time for all of the Connecticut State Correctional Facility for women since, the population, having grown to over one thousand female inmates, it could no longer be classified as a correctional facility. As a result, all of the rules and regulations were immediately converted to the standards equal with the men's state prisons. We were informed that all of our personal clothing would have to be sent out or thrown out and that we would no longer be allowed to have food sent into us from our families. The only items we were permitted to keep were one pair of slippers, white sneakers, a white colored robe, grey sweat pants, white tee shirts, and white undergarments. Our appliance items could be retained, but when they broke, they had to be discarded. All food items had to be purchased from the facility's commissary store.

To add insult to injury, every inmate was to be issued three state uniforms, nightwear and a pair of heavy work boots. No jewelry was permitted with the exception of a watch and a religious metal. All other necessary items would be eventually available for purchase at the state-run commissary. Of course the new changes took effect before the facility found vendors to supply necessities, and it was a couple of months before inmates could buy such items. The institution did notify each of us, that in the future they would institute special programs for all inmates that remained charge free within the facility, including specialty food packages from selected vendors of the facility's choice. If an inmate remained free of all institutional infractions, they would then be permitted to place a food order at the specified time.

The institutional changes did save the facility a lot of work and man power since previously each item that came into the institution had to be searched, stamped with the inmate's state prison number and packaged for each person, before being transported to the different housing units with the result that drug-addicted inmates were always crafting new ways to smuggle in drugs, stuffing them into the lining of a coat or inside the soles of a sneaker. But the change affected many of us adversely. No longer did our clothing reflect the possibility that we would soon become part of the general population. The other inmates never again mistook me for a staff member.

Soon after the facility's dramatic changes, I was called up to the administration building to be informed that they had found the prison's battered women group quilt project so impressive that they had hung the quilt on display in the administration's boardroom with the result that someone from the governor's office contacted Mrs. Watson and requested that the quilt be displayed at his, as well as being sent on tour to New London and Middlesex Counties. It seems that our project was about to connect to society in a big way and my picture was taken standing next to the finished project. I was also given photos of the Assistant Administrator posing next to the quilt. I was so thrilled to have the collective expression of so many women make a mark in the community.

Entertainment was always a morale booster. Now, we had weekend movies and the theater group plays to look forward to seeing. Unfortunately, the theater group would no longer be permitted to continue productions, because of the stipulated uniform clothing regulation which did not allow any inmate to wear civilian clothing a regulation, all of which gave me an idea for a new play, *The Colorful Quilt* in which all the actors would wear state issued jump suits, so that there would not be any violation of the new instituted clothing rules. My hope was to enlighten many of the prisoners that didn't have an understanding of domestic violence, as well as the public. It also served as an aid to help connect the women that had suffered terrible abuse in their lives.

The collaboration of the all of the inmates in the theater guild was outstanding. All of the women that joined used their skills to help in the production of the play. Some of them cut cardboard, while others painted the props to resemble prison scenery. Dana was the director of the play. She organized all of the rehearsals and planned out each scene. Other women controlled the stage lights and audio microphones. Some inmates were in charge of the timing of each curtain call, in between acts, while others designed and created the playbill. The play, which was based on my own life, ran for two consecutive nights, and all of the minimum-security prisoners attended the show. The play was so successful that Mrs. Watson asks for the play to be performed in a daytime production for various battered women's organizations from communities in Connecticut Domestic Violence shelters.

As I walked out onto the stage for a curtain call, my eyes locked on those of a women sitting center stage, about five rows back from the stage whose eyes were bruised. Clearly, she had recently suffered terrible abuse, and I was awestruck by the fact that she was attending our play. I was so hopeful that our situation would help her never to return to her abuser again. Just that one connection made all of our efforts worthwhile.

Later, the Administration allowed our theater group to perform for our families which was such an emotional experience since each and every person in the audience understood the messages clearly. The reality of the theme resided in each individual's heart, and I will never forget the warmth of my daughter's embrace after the performance.

The holidays came and went and another year passed as I welcomed the up-coming New Year. It was 2000, the millennium year, a milestone in our history, and even though I was not yet free, I reveled in the fact that I might mark this year as my next to last year held in captivity. I had high hopes for all great things to happen. It had been four years since my clemency petition had been submitted to governor's office.

On January 31, 2000, Connecticut's governor, who was leaving office, denied my clemency petition in a form letter. Needless to say, after all I had done, I was completely devastated, as were Naomi, Babs, Rabbi Jacob and Paula. Each one of these individuals had worked so hard to help me.

My hardest task was telling my daughter the terrible news. I wanted to fall apart but I knew that I had to be the stronger one for the two of us. For Marie's sake, I had to down play it as if it had been a long shot but that my fight would continue.

Despite this disappointment, parole was around the corner. I definitely would be home soon. It gave us solace during a very bleak time. I counted on the system and their fairness. There was a light at the end of the tunnel. For the first time since incarceration, I could see that far ahead.

TWENTY-TWO

Puppy Love Supersedes Corruption

THE DAYS TRUDGED ONWARD AND I managed to pull up my bootstraps and continue to assume a facade of normalcy. Good friend, Dana, had been granted parole, having served fifteen years of imprisonment and was going to be parole supervised for the rest of her life. She left the institution with glee in her eyes. I felt sad to have her go, although I was happy for her freedom. And since, at that time, I was the only other inmate who was knowledgeable when it came to the audio video equipment, I took over the audio-video setup for all institutional movies, assembles and events that were held in the gymnasium. Every Friday and Saturday evening, I would go over to the gym and set up the sound system, behind the stage area.

On March 17, 2000, on Saint Patrick's Day evening, I set up the sound system for movie night. It was an ordinary evening like all the others and so I returned to my unit and waited for the movie to end when I could return to shut down the sound system. It was about ten o'clock when I returned to the educational building. I checked in with. Officer Stein, a toned, tattooed fellow of German descent who was posted on the floor of the building that evening, and thought little of it when he followed me into the gym to turn off the audio equipment. But when it was time for me to leave and he blocked my way, I began to be nervous, and when he put his arms around me, I freaked out. Still, frightened and vulnerable as he made me feel, I pushed him away and told him he was a disgrace to his uniform, after which I marched back to my cottage and reported him to Officer Rose.

Interviews with other officials followed, reminding me all too vividly of the past and the retaliation that might follow. But instead, Officer Stein disappeared and this incident set a tone for all of the other correctional officers in that facility. The word around the compound was to not harass Ms. Viola which really helped me to secure respect from every officer that valued their uniform, and the code of ethics they had sworn to follow when wearing it. Remembering how my incarceration had begun, I was aware that I had reached a higher level emotionally. Consequently I never had another incident involving an officer or an inmate, the remaining length of my incarceration.

Inside the prison there had been numerous incidents of officer corruption but now the days of prison guard power and control over prisoners, seemed to come to a halt. An internal crackdown had been implemented for many months, and as a result, various offending officers, higher ranking officials and staff members were arrested and escorted from the institution, and charged with criminal accusations, including rape, sexual assault and other related offenses. It was a period of time filled with transformation within the prison, targeting the corrupt individuals that held positions of power. These positive changes were a long time coming and desperately needed.

By the middle of the summer more changes in my life materialized. I was called out of work to the Administration Building for an interview for a new program that was being brought into our facility, a privately funded prison program initiated originally in the New York Prison System called Paws Behind Bars which featured seven-week-old puppies that were specially breed at the Guide Dog Agency. These puppies would live at the prison with an inmate who would train them for a period of twelve to eighteen months, preparing them to become guide dogs for the blind.

The puppy program was the most exciting I had encountered yet. I met with Gail Stoge, the founder of Paws Behind Bars, and Mr. Henson the prison's Assistant Administer. Gail had a thin body frame but a powerful personality. Every inmate had to have an infraction free record while at the institution and be within twelve months of parole.

Once accepted, I learned that I would have my puppy twenty-four hours a day, during which time we would receive training which would prepare the dog for Puppy College to be taught to become a guide dog for the blind. I was so thrilled to be considered for participation in such an awesome program because I knew that these puppies would bring love and light into my world. The gifts I could receive from a baby puppy would be immeasurable.

The mere fact of being able to touch the coat of these animals was intensely gratifying. It had been over six years since, with the exception of visits with my loved ones, I had had any intimate human contact. Until that moment, I hadn't realized just how my environment had affected me. I couldn't wait to hold a baby puppy and I made it my job to learn every lesson Gail offered. I wanted to be at the top of my class and receive my own little ball of fur to nurture and love.

During the morning puppy class Gail taught us everything we needed to know about dog behavior and anatomy. We learned how these special puppies were bred and what part we would be taking in their lives. The puppies would be depended on us for all of their needs. We would be responsible for house breaking, obedience training, exercising, and socialization and minor medical treatments. Each week we had to cut their nails, clean their ears and brush their coats. Whenever necessary, we were responsible for treating them with medications and first aid. The puppies would receive around the clock care and training. Women who were assigned, as a primary puppy raisers would have a puppy living in their cell. Those puppies would go to work with us every day.

The breeding process at the Guide Dog Agency was so finely tuned that they were able to breed out most medical and temperament issues, but the confidence building, was dependent upon raising the puppy properly. It was our job to help that puppy grow into a confident canine which would hopefully one day become the eyes of a person without sight.

When I was chosen as a trainer, I couldn't wait to call home to tell my daughter the great news. I told her that she would get to meet the puppy on our visits. During my weekly abuse counseling, I shared my excitement with my therapist, Paula, who, understanding, as she did, the complexity of how beneficial this puppy would be in my life couldn't wait to meet my new addition and even sent the news to Naomi for me. I was so excited about my new journey back into a feeling, loving and caring individual that I wanted to tell the entire world the wonderful news. It was a freedom for me, a release of some many suppressed emotions and physical limitations imposed on me through my incarceration. Jake, my eight-week-old tiny black Labrador, transformed my life.

The four women that were selected as puppy raisers were given two weeks off from all institutional work schedules. The purpose behind this was twofold, to bond with our new puppy and house-break them completely. Our rooms were equipped with a dog kennel, food and water bowls, and toys. The wing was sectioned off, with a dog gate at one end of the hallway, and an exit to the puppy yard at the other, complete with slides and platforms for them to climb on, as well as picnic tables where we trainers could sit and watch them.

The two weeks of bonding was the most incredible experience. I nurtured that puppy as if he was my newborn baby. Jake was the calmest puppy in the group. He was super easy to housebreak and he recognized his name by the end of our bonding period. I had tremendous success of our method of training. Every command was only voiced once and the puppies were rewarded, with praise instead of food, a particularly clever idea since the dog would obey us even if we were out of treats, reinforcing their natural instinct to please us.

In the following months I went to work at the law office with Jake in tow, and was amazed at the instantaneous change in atmosphere. These puppies brought with them a lightheartedness that would have never happened without their presence. Jake was happy to sit on his pillow underneath my desk. In between my legal interviews, I took him out to "get busy," during which time he always receiving a stroke from some passerby. It was so refreshing to have Jake by my side. He was truly my best friend. He always listened and never judged me. His was pure and innocent love without expectations. Jake totally changed my life in such a profound way. I felt as though I was in a good dream instead of a nightmare.

When Jake was four months old, he was able to respond to commands almost one hundred percent of the time. The administrators, definitely impressed and satisfied with the puppy program, decided to have various administrators attend a brief demonstration o which included the puppy handlers showing off their well-behaved canines. Jake's behavior was amazing that day. This four month old puppy obeyed commands that most dogs of full age could never attain. Jake walked on my left side without the slightest pulling. He sat on command, went into a down position when I instructed him to do so and didn't move from that position when I told him to stay. His concentration on me and my commands was absolute. I was so very proud of my four-month-old furry baby.

Puppy class was truly growling, but worth every second. Gail's criticism when we showed her our training skills was so helpful. She wanted us to be perfect in every way. During our class, the other women in the program would practice their training techniques on Jake and the other puppies. We taught them to walk over uneven surfaces like street grates, sandy terrain, wet grassy areas and hard blacktop to prepare them to guide their owners no matter where they went. We had to write lengthy puppy care letters, for the outside volunteers who would keep the dogs over the weekends. In these letters, we would describe our dog's personality traits I couldn't imagine saying goodbye to this creature when the time, as it must, arrived. I pushed the sad thought out of my head and tried to absorb all the joy Jake brought into my life each and every day.

When Jake turned ten months old, Gail decided that, since I had done an excellent job raising him, it was time for him to be given to an alternate and brought me a puppy named Merry whose raiser was having difficulty teaching her obedience techniques. I was sad to let Jake go, but I knew that Merry needed my help. Still, I didn't know what to expect, and as human beings, we always expect the worst, when the unknown is ahead of us.

On the morning of Merry's arrival my nervous energy was at an all-time high, particularly as it was the custom for new pups to be introduced to all the others, and at first glance, I could see that Merry was beyond high energy. Pulling wildly on her leash as she approached us, with an ear-to-ear puppy smile, her tongue hanging out, she could have been a small sled dog. When she jumped on me, she almost knocked me down. But as wild and crazy as this little dog was she possessed an infectious happiness and energy that I loved even though I could see that we had a huge amount of work ahead of us.

For the first couple of days with Merry, I questioned my puppy training skills. She was a true test of patience and consistency. But she was intelligent. When she obeyed I praised her and allowed her to continue her playtime, calculating that, if I continued to challenge her energy level, her training would prove a success. Merry and I created a bond that would last a lifetime.

The puppy program had volunteers from the community that would take them to their homes on the weekend to socialize them and build confidence. When I told Naomi about the program, she volunteered to be a weekend puppy sitter bringing one home for the weekend to socialize them out in the community. She not only enjoyed having the puppies each weekend, but was totally amazed at their obedience training. Naomi's puppy experience prompted her to adopt a released dog from the guide dog agency. This was a program that benefited everyone it touched.

Months later, Merry had apparently had been released from guide school because of a medical condition. Since guide dogs had to be one hundred percent healthy, this condition disqualified her from becoming a guild dog. Naomi didn't tell me that the Guide Dog Agency picked Merry for her to adopt; instead she showed up a week later at an institution assembly with Merry. When I walked into the gymnasium to set up the audio video equipment and saw Merry sitting next to Naomi, we locked eyes, and she started to wiggle with excitement until Naomi gave her the command, "You're free," whereupon Merry immediately ran toward me, her paws sliding on the gym floor. As she jumped up in a licking frenzy, I was thrilled to have her back in my arms.

Twenty-Three

Parole Board Hearing

On December 27, 2001, I finally became eligible for parole. After seven years and eleven months of imprisonment, I was scheduled for my parole hearing on November 7, a date that marked a new horizon in my journey toward freedom, a path that I had assiduously paved with achievements which I was certain would make me eligible.

I awoke that morning with such anticipation that my stomach could not handle any food or water. My nerves were on edge and my mind raced with a million random thoughts. I didn't have any idea what to expect at my parole hearing. I only knew that I would present myself, as the person I had grown to be. Rabbi Jacob had informed Naomi, Babs and Paula of the great news and I had arranged for my parole plans to include my residence at the Women's Abuse Center Transitional Housing Program for a period of one year. Everything seemed set to go. My program information was pre-approved and set for my release and Rabbi Jacob had told me he would be at the institution when my hearing was over to get all the particulars of the parole panel's decision.

Breathless almost to the point of hyperventilation, I found myself facing a Loni Farris, and a man named Juan Rodriquez who, the moment he said, "You are not the victim here," let me know I was up against enemy fire, about to be engaged in a psychological warfare for which I was totally unprepared. The two-parole panel-hearing officers aggressively fired questions at me one after another. Before I had the opportunity to fully answer one question, one of them would abruptly interrupt me and then he or she would finish answering the question with their own opinion of what they believed happened in my case, taking turns interrupting and rebutting all of my responses.

Mr. Rodriquez was especially cruel and augmentative. The more I continued to tell my truth about my part in my criminal offense, or my life experience leading up to the crime, Mr. Rodriquez became angrier, and angrier, playing the role of judge, jury and executor, accusing me of crimes that were never a part of my record, and when I protested, became enraged. And soon it became apparent that they both had preconceived ideas of what had happened.

At the end of three hours of mental and emotional torture, the two man panel denied my parole release, and gave me an estimated future parole eligibility date of thirty-six months, basing their decision, as far as I could see, not on my accomplishments while incarcerated, but on the arbitrary decision of the Superior Court Judge years ago.

I walked out of that parole hearing room a broken person, and sobbed my heart out to Rabbi Jacobs who was waiting in the foyer and immediately conveyed the news to Naomi and Babs, both of whom, although not familiar with the guidelines of the parole process, were certain that a grave injustice had occurred in my case. Babs was especially exasperated about these sensitive abuse issues that she fought so diligently to make law in our State Legislation.

Despite the tragedy of my parole hearing, I continued to live out each day with some sort of purpose, interviewing women that were given the opportunity of parole release. Some of these women had never held a real job. Others had violated parole already and returned to the prison system a second and third time. They had committed violent crimes and had terrible institutional records and yet, in spite of their record, had been granted parole, illustrating the same disparity that can be seen in the judicial system in general. Given what had happened to me, I had every right to be bitter, and I suppose I was, but I was committed to establishing justice in the system.

Babs was about to begin her own quest for justice on my behalf. She had vowed to help me four years earlier and her intentions were still as fresh as they had been on the first day we had met. To this end, she contacted an attorney by the name of Ted Roma who was not only a member of the Women's Abuse Center Board of Trustees, and a certified trial attorney who argued cases in front of the state's supreme court, but also a personal friend of Babs. And after my being vetted by his paralegal, he agreed to take my case.

My next meeting was the following week when Ted came to interview me, accompanied by Babs. His confidence and conviction reassured me that he was someone I could trust since he was a true professional in every sense of the word. According to his words, Ted was going to fight this miscarriage of justice and because of him, my will to fight for the "freedom" I had earned returned.

Mr. Ted Roma appealed the decision of denial of parole to the board immediately. It was the beginning to an extensive process filled with tactics of mishandling. The parole agency displayed their ultra-powers in paper shuffling, and purposeful delays. In fact, the parole board violated every rule within their reach, to discourage my request. Every failure to comply with their legal criteria caused me to be detained within the prison longer. It proved to be the practice of the parole board, to play legal games in order to achieve this, in some case to such an extent that the state's Superior Court Appellate Division was forced to intercede.

The parole board ignored Mr. Roma's parole appeal until late February, 2002, at which time it was denied because he had, they claimed, failed to submit a reconsideration of their decision, a document which he had not received. And when he finally did, it took them over fifty days to respond, reaffirming their decision, although amending the wording of the reasons for their denial, and when he appealed, called for a "DeNovo hearing" which was, in effect, a review of their previous decision.

On August 26, 2002, I was called to the Educational Building for my second parole hearing only to encounter Mr. Rodriquez and Ms. Farris, the very same hearing officers that held my original hearing and once again, after a prolonged chess game in which I was presented as a monster, this "new" parole panel once again denied my parole, and gave me a twenty-seven month future eligibility date for parole consideration.

At that moment, I knew that if I didn't succeed in the Superior Court of Connecticut, I would remain in prison for the full duration of my original sentence. The parole board panel's written decision still hadn't been forwarded to my attorneys or to the Superior Court Appellate Division. I had a sinking feeling that the fight for my freedom was about to get tougher. My hands were tied and I could do absolutely nothing to avoid whatever fate they had planned for me. I didn't have the knowledge of the power the parole board panel actually had, or the magnitude of their power. Ted Roma again submitted a motion to proceed on appeal, without a parole board panel's written decision for the reason they had denied parole, a motion which, although this denied the decision of the Superior Court of Connecticut Appellate Division which had directed the Parole Board Panel to submit a written decision within twenty days.

I thought this was great news. The court was demanding the parole board to produce documentation in support of the parole denial. My attorney could not proceed on appeal in the Connecticut court system without that written decision. With the court's demand that the parole board panel provide a written decision, the panel decided once again to vacate my second parole hearing in lieu of a court battle on appeal. The fact that they vacated my second parole decision meant more foot dragging and time stalling, on the part of the parole panel. The next method of retaliation from the parole panel was to order me to endure an in-depth psychological evaluation that the panel determined they needed to aid in determining my eligibility for parole. The parole board expedited the in-depth examine to take place prior to my third parole consideration hearing.

On December 9, 2002, the parole panel submitted a motion to dismiss my appeal of parole denial for reasons of "Failure to Exhaust Administrative Remedies". On January 7, 2003, the Connecticut Superior Court Appellate Division denied the parole board panel's motion and again ordered them to provide a written decision for denial of parole. In the middle of January 2003, I was summoned to the Administration Building to undergo an in-depth psychological evaluation following the parole panel's decision to vacate. I spoke with Mr. Roma and he advised me to do whatever they ask of me, although the parole panel had violated a Superior Court's Order dated January 7, 2003. Once again the Connecticut Superior Court Appellate Division wrote an order for the parole board panel to submit a written decision of my parole denial.

At that stage in time, I was legally considered a ward of the court, and it was out of the parole board panel's scope of power to deny parole, whereupon the panel took it upon themselves, to ignore the Superior Court's Order completely. As an inmate, I didn't have a choice to refuse any in-depth examination nor a third parole board panel hearing. I had to comply or be placed in lock up. I was, I realized, a true victim of the parole board panel's vicious game.

On January 31, 2003, after another exhausting but thorough psychological examination, I was again called for my third parole panel hearing, this time watching and participating via video camera which was a relief to me since being distanced in this way made me feel less violated, particularly when I discovered that my old foe, Ms. Farris, was in charge of the hearing.

This particular parole panel hearing lasted only fifteen minutes during which I was forced to listen, despite my denials, to a series of incorrect facts. Perhaps the most blatant error was their claim that I had been tried, an assertion they clung onto even when I reminded them that, actually, I had taken a plea bargain. When I was given another thirty-six month parole eligibility date for parole consideration. I was not surprised and clearly not devastated because it was an expected result. I had been through such a mental warfare, with this parole board panel that refused to acknowledge their power over me and notified my attorney, Mr. Roma, of the way in which Mrs. Farris had orchestrated the proceedings, a claim which he included in my next appeal.

In March 2003, when my attorney had yet to receive a written decision from the parole board panel, Mr. Roma was outraged that the board had ignored the psychiatrist's recommendation that I be released, with the result that the court scheduled an oral hearing of my appeal for the date of June 3, 2003. On that date the parole board panel still had not submitted their written decision. During that oral argument, the court gave the parole panel another order to produce their decision in writing within nine days. The parole board panel finally had no other alternative but to submit the written decision to the Connecticut Superior Court Appellate Division, on June 12, 2003.

Ted Roma, Babs and Naomi decided to not inform me of the scheduled date for my appeal's oral argument for June 3, 2003. In their opinion, I had been so often disappointed in the battle of freedom with parole board panel that they couldn't bring me more anxiety by letting me know that the oral argument was taking place. They were in agreement that, pending the outcome of the oral argument, I would then be informed of the adjudication, but not a minute sooner. As a result, I went about my prison life without knowing my life was about to change at the hands of the three Court Justices that sat on the Superior Court of Connecticut's Appellate Division Bench. At that juncture I had so many disappointments regarding the legal system my hope for freedom was exhausted.

Twenty-Four

Superior Court Appeal Release

On June 18, 2003, I was instructed to go the Administration Building to receive a call from my attorney. Heart racing, I listened to the man I had come to know as Ted ask me if I was sitting down. And when I said that I was, he said the magic words. I was a free woman at last "We did it," he told me. "The Superior Court decided on your case and an order has been written that you be released from prison forthwith which means that you are to be released immediately."

I screamed with excitement and jumped around the room. The entire floor of civilian workers came rushing into that office. I guess they thought that I had terrible news, and were ready to pin me down in a chokehold to control my emotional outburst. But when I told them that I was finally a free woman, they hugged me instead. It was the happiest moment in my life.

Until that phone call, I was unaware that the Superior Court Appellate Division had finally received the parole board panel's written decision. After a review of the record of my appeal was examined, the court rendered their decision to reverse the parole board panel's decision. They did so with a written order stating the court's decision to reverse my parole denial and provide for my immediate release which had come so suddenly and so unexpectedly that it might as well have been the parting of the Red Sea, particularly since the usual procedure was to send it back to the parole board for them to correct the error, the court system usually being unlikely to delve into agency matters of that kind. It was understandable then that

I should consider my immediate release from prison clearly nothing short of a miracle.

I am certain that the administrators were at a lost for what to do next. It was not every day that the Superior Court released an inmate immediately. Given that, it was no wonder that the authorities were forced to search for the proper formalities. As for me, the key word was "Forthwith," meant, "Now!" Unfortunately, it soon became apparent that the institution didn't regard my release with the same urgency which I did.

When I was told to go down to the basement floor of the Administration Building and report to the parole office, I was shaking from nervousness which turned to absolute terror when, once there, I saw Ms. Farris march past the desk where I was waiting for the exit paperwork. Although she did not so much as glance at me, it was clear that she was furious, and I could hear her, once she was in her office, questioning the validity of the order. Clutching my preliminary exit papers close to my breast, I ran back to the cottage, and, eager to make this all seem as real as possible, called Marie who, a few days later, would turn twenty-five.

"I'm free!" I cried when she answered the phone. "I won my appeal! Happy birthday, my child! This is your early present!"

At that we both broke into tears and it was some time before I could compose myself to tell her that I wanted her to be the one at the prison gate, to pick me up. I made her aware that the parole office had to finish my exit paperwork, and I would call her when it was time to come. That phone call was placed early afternoon on June 18, 2003, the day the court order was dated for my immediate release.

After informing my cottage's officer of the news and receiving her congratulations, I spent two hours cleaning out all of my things, but by four o'clock, count time had come and gone and I still had not heard from the authorities about my release. It so happened, that my puppy, Jim, would be leaving the next morning for a puppy swap with the New York prison puppy handlers. I already had the alternate puppy handler on call to take my dog in the event the administration ever called me for release that day or evening. At about five o'clock I again called Marie and told her that it was getting late and I still hadn't heard anything about my release. She was so upset that the prison was holding me after the court had released me that she said that she was going to call the prison administrator and also my attorney which she did only to discover that, thanks to a glitch concerning the paper work, I would have to wait until the next morning. This development, thanks to the determination of my arch enemy, Ms. Farris, filled me with terror.

After tossing and turning all night, I rose at six o'clock in the morning, convinced that I would never get out of that prison. I walked Jim, my latest puppy, and fed him his breakfast, before writing an updated puppy letter, telling his new raiser in New York about his commands. It was ironic that Jim was set to leave the same day I was being released. I wondered if he would miss me when he returned. Knowing that he must have been aware of my tension during the past twenty-four hours, I had a little one-on-one talk with him, explaining that he and I would have to part ways and that he would always be in my heart. I thanked him for all the love he gave me in the short time we had together, and told him we were both off to bigger and better things in life, and that, although our paths would separate, he would always be a big part of my life. It was a bittersweet goodbye. I walked him down the hallway to the alternate puppy handler's room. I then proceeded to take all of my belonging and give them away, to all the other puppy raisers.

I wanted nothing but the sweat suit I was wearing. Television, radio, tee shirts, everything went out of that room with whomever grabbed it first. In the middle of trashing the rest of my unwanted things, I was called to the officer's desk to be informed that it was time for my exit medical examination which would be administered at the maximum-security hospital, something that was, understandably, a tension-filled experience, particularly since I had hoped never to enter that building again.

I just made it back to my cottage in time for eleven o'clock count time only to find that my release papers still had not arrived. And then, as I sat on my bed, waiting to be counted for what I could only hope was the last time, suddenly our cottage mouse, Charlie, ran under my door as though he had come to say goodbye. I was still laughing hysterically when I heard my name called and I was told to go to the exit building. Immediately, I screamed with joy and all the women in the cottage clapped and cheered for me. As I left the cottage all of them, together with my cottage officer, came along to watch me walk to freedom. It was pure joy, and I could only wish that my mother had been alive to witness my release.

And then I realized that my mother was already there, smiling down from heaven at me, enjoying the fact that finally justice had been done. By the time, I was on my way down "The Freedom Road," which was off limits for all the inmates, tears were streaming down my face as I was overwhelmed with the realization that at last I was truly free.

As I approached the top of the hill, I saw the front gates of the prison. I had been to this gate dozens of times with my puppies for volunteers to pick them up but they had always been locked to me. Now, however, my daughter Marie, my grandson Karl and my youngest sister Clara were waiting for me. Crying so hard that it was difficult to see, I ran through the gate and hugged them each so hard that I thought I would break them in half.

It was overwhelming just to be riding free in a car. Marie handed me her flip top cell phone and I didn't even know how to open it. It was such a foreign object to me that I was hesitant to even touch it. I had had no idea what I had missed during the past ten years. All of a sudden I was in a giant world, and I felt so small. Simultaneously, it was all very wonderful and frightening.

Our first stop was at Ted Roma's office in Norwich where both Ted Roma and his staff greeted me with enthusiasm and warmth. Ted wanted me to know that the Head Presiding Judge had told the State's Attorney that the parole board panel had made a mockery out of their agency, but that she would not allow them to make a mockery out of her courtroom, and that the court would write a legal opinion of my case to be published in the Connecticut Superior Court Reports law book, finally validated my victimization. He was so kind and sincere that it touched my heart.

Our next stop was my new home at the Women's Abuse Center where Naomi, Babs, Paula, Rabbi Jacob and many other staff members from the women's center greeted us hosted a small party for me and, as an extra treat, Merry welcomed me with a thorough face licking. After that I was taken to the woman's shelter where I was to stay for sixty days before being transferred to the transitional house for an additional ten months. In that sixty-day time span, I had to secure full time employment and obtain a vehicle. On my first day it felt like a very tall order of accomplishments especially, since I didn't even have any identification at that point in time.

My first night at the shelter was a sleepless one, in a strange environment for me, made more poignant by the pain Marie had so obviously felt in not being able to take me home with her at once. As for me, I spent most of the night playing my exodus over and over again in my mind too afraid, to go to sleep for fear of waking up and finding myself still confined in prison instead of being in this comfortable rural setting in which, although I was expected to do chores, the emphasis was on my return as a citizen to the real world.

There were rules, of course, including the requirement of showing proof of payment of fines, weekly meetings with my parole officer, a ban on alcohol consumption, and random drug testing. Most important, perhaps, was the fact that leaving the state was absolutely forbidden. When, some days later, Babs was driving me to a restaurant which she had described as an old church now converted into a center of gourmet delight, I, at the last minute, realized that if we were to drive a few more miles, we would be in Rhode Island.

Later it was Babs who wrote me a letter written from a Washington D.C. hotel dated June 18, 2003 which read:

> **Dear Margo:**
>
> **By the time you receive this, you will have hear the wonderful news. I'm in Washington on business and since all day I had you on my mind, I came back to my hotel and called Ted to see if he had heard anything. He said had received a phone call that the opinion was officially published. I said, "I can feel your joy". Margo I just wanted you to know what a privilege it had been to be a part of fighting for your freedom. You have been down a long and difficult road and now you will have the opportunity to travel down a new path. You have had courage and dignity throughout your incarceration and I know that you will continue to be strong as you reclaim your life. After I talked to Ted, I went for a walk to the Capital and thought about all the great events I have witnessed in that building and in this city. I thought about the values and meaning of our country and our system of democracy and justice. It**

> **doesn't always work, but today it did. I cried for your joy for you and praised God for his blessings.**
>
> **Sincerely, Babs**

This letter will be inscribed in my heart and mind forever. How fortunate I was to have connected with this woman, to have had her as my front-line warrior, in the battle for my life.

The Superior Court of Connecticut, Appellate Division wrote a court opinion after deciding my appeal. This legal documentation was published in *The Superior Court Record,* which is a hardbound reference book containing legal case law. Attorneys use these published cases to support their legal argument, in presenting their case to the court. The gifts I received from this this publication were twofold. First, I was so pleased that the parole board panel would be preventing from treating other freedom-worthy individuals, with their arbitrary treatment. Secondly, I felt that the highest authorities had finally validated my life experience. Now, at last, I could begin my journey of emotional healing. This appellate opinion was a true gift to me on so many levels.

Still, my attorney thought it was necessary to file a motion against the state which, when it was refused, became the subject of an article by *The Post Current Magazine* explaining the basis for a former Superior Court Judge, John D'Angelo, having been appointed to conduct a full audit of the parole agency's operations to ensure that its decisions in future were not influenced by politics or other outside influences. A parole agency would also implement a four-member panel to review all policy and procedures governing prisoner's releases and stated that these dramatic parole changes took place after the Superior Court of Connecticut Appellate Division reversed a parole decision of denial of parole for a Connecticut woman, Margo Viola Saunders.

Meanwhile, I continued my journey to rebuild my life, beginning with applying for employment at any number of the small businesses in the quaint little town where I was now living. And since, on some of the applications, it clearly asks if I was ever convicted of a felony, my heart skipped a beat, as I filled in my answer. It was the first time during my short period of freedom that I came to realize my job search might well be more difficult than I had expected, and I remember pedaling back to the women's shelter, with tears streaming down my face.

After that, I made myself a deal; I gave myself permission to feel melancholy on those bike rides only, although I do remember the desperation I felt when not one of the businesses out of the dozens of applications I had submitted, called me. I still continued to take my bike rides into town and fill out more job requests. I believed that, if I filled out enough job applications, someone would eventually give me a chance.

And, in the end, I had offers from a beauty salon and from a veterinarian hospital, but the big surprise came when my attorney whom I now called Ted offered me a position in his office as a legal secretary.

In my heart I think that Ted went through the interview process to give me a sense of pride and dignity. I don't think he read anything on my resume, nor do I think he cared about my certification. He was so kind in pretending that he was interested in my legal experience. I believe that Ted Roma intended to give me a job because he felt for my situation, and wanted me to succeed. The office was small, with one office manager, four paralegals and two legal secretaries, and I was welcomed with open arms. It was a warm safe environment, filled with individuals who were familiar with every aspect of my life. Each one of the people who were employed by this firm was genuinely happy I had joined the staff. It was so refreshing to have such a friendly working environment.

As I exited Ted's office, I was enveloped in the unpretentiousness of the surroundings in my new world. My thoughts reflected the multitude of possibilities introduced to me, and I was overwhelmed with tremendous gratitude.

TWENTY-FIVE

Battered Women's Transitional Program

I WAS AWESTRUCK BY THE next phase in the program the transitional house, an enormous estate that was set on several acres that faced a horse farm. The view from the outside deck was magnificent. It had two large kitchens and eleven separate bedrooms, each with a private full bathroom.

The property was private and secluded from the bustle of the busy town. It also was connected with the safe house facility and the location was a secret for the protection of the battered women and their children. Families could live there free from fear of their abusers and have a fair amount of time to gain a life of independence in a serene environment. Only a few women were living there when I joined them, but I was impressed by the fact that they came from such diverse backgrounds. There were well-educated professionals and struggling mothers but everyone had the same common story of a torturous life filled with abuse. Some of the women struggled with family court protection order and child custody battles. Others didn't have children and were on the run from their significant other. There were so many resources to smooth our way back into society.

Now that I had managed to achieve my short-term goals on the path of self-sufficiency, my next order of business was to establish long term goals that would allow me to relocate, when the time came, closer to my daughter, grandson and friends, and with that in mind, my first step was to open an one-on-one dog obedience training company, one of my first customers being Ted and his wife who brought me their beautiful female golden retriever, Sandy, to train.

It was a busy time. Monday through Fridays I worked as a legal secretary and also trained Sandy. Two evening a week I had meetings and obligations for the housing program and once a week I attended private one-on-one psychological therapy with a private psychiatrist, leaving me just enough time for my puppy training business as well as spending a few hours each week in an upscale consignment shop from which I volunteered. I also bought my own clothes there, which allowed me to contribute financially to the Women's Abuse Center, to help more women in distress.

In the meantime, my daughter Marie and Taylor her finance, were planning their wedding for August 26, 2003. My daughter's boyfriend, Taylor O'Hearn, had proposed to her a year prior to my being released from prison. They had lived together for several years and had recently purchased a home in Darien. Taylor, a fourth grade school teacher at the Darien Upper Elementary School, was a responsible man in his early thirties, who gave my daughter the stability and love she so badly needed.

Marie had wanted to wait for my freedom in order to actually have a wedding ceremony with her mother present, and I was eager to contribute whatever I could to the occasion, with the result that I contacted a long term friend, Ron Holman, a disk jockey, who was delighted to provide the music. Another friend, Lenny, a collector of unique vehicles, provided the Cadillac in which we would be driven to the wedding.

As the mother-of-the bride, I watched with pride as Marie became the wife of a man I was sure would make her happy. Even the appearance of Scott, which came as no surprise, did not unnerve me, and I was pleased that he had the opportunity to see me as the new woman I had become.

The excitement, I found, was far from coming to an end. The next week the Women's Abuse Center, inviting me to this special event they were hosting at a hotel in Norwich, one at which Ted Roma was to be a special honorary recipient of an award, for all his voluntary good works done for the women's center. It occurred on a Sunday evening and I, along with all the girls at the law office, were invited to sit at the head table during this special event. It was an honor and a miracle to be present. It was the most incredible feeling to be at the honoree's head table among all of the individuals who attended that evening, including, to my surprise, the Connecticut State Correctional Facility's Head Administrator, Mrs. Watson, Assistant Administrators, Mr. Wallace Henson and Mr. Karnel and other staff members of the prison facility. It was, I thought, ironic that a former felon was seated at the honoree's head table and the big important people were seated in the back of the room.

After that evening I felt really bonded to the Roma family, and the entire positive influence their presence had had in my life. Ted Roma's wife, Lena, a police detective became one of my close friends. Together with them and the people in his office who welcomed me with open arms, I felt like a true member of the community. Lena and Ted had a windbreaker made with the puppy business's name embroidered on the front. It was so special and extremely considerate for them to put so much thought into my gift, and I appreciated it, just as I did being invited to every family celebration they had. I had given their three-year-old daughter, Sarah her first real haircut, and both Lena and Ted became clients, as well.

I took such great pride and pleasure in being welcomed into their family that anything I could do to show them my appreciation was too small a task. One day, having been charmed by a handbag made from a wooden cigar box. I visited the local cigar shop and ask the owner if he had any discarded cigar boxes, after which I went to a craft store and bought cloth, beads, jewels, wire and crystal diamonds and I decorated six of them, lining the insides with the cloth, and drilling holes in the top for the beaded handle I made by stringing the beads with wire. I finished the boxes by gluing the crystal diamonds on the outside as well as placing a tassel around the beaded handle. Everyone who received one of these, including Marie, Lena and Ted, were impressed by my creativity.

Since the holiday season was fast approaching, I took that opportunity to begin my journey toward making my way back to my hometown. Once I had completed my eight month stay the Women's Abuse Center, I would need a full-time job, and so it was then I got in touch with my former boss, Mel, at La Mes Salon who, when he finally called back after leaving me waiting for weeks, suggested that I remain in the paralegal and puppy training field, after adding that his staff was not particularly enthusiastic about a former felon being employed.

I remained silent for a few seconds, before I found voice enough to thank him for his consideration and hung up immediately before the knot in my throat choked me to death, reduced to tears, crushed in a way that I never expected or thought would happen. Suddenly my self-confidence sank so low that I believed that I would never recover. I imagined that the entire community of Darien must have felt the same way and that my quest to return to that area was doomed.

As the holiday season approached, I found it difficult to feel like celebrating despite the fact that the women's center had adopted my family and sent Marie and Karl wonderful holiday gifts to open in my name. I was so awestruck by their kindness and generosity that it convinced me to never give up on my dreams. There were great people out in the world that would offer me a second chance, to fulfill my desire for reuniting with my family. I just had to build courage enough, to reach out to as many as I could and eventually someone would invite me into their world. I thought of the clichés my mother had been fond of repeating: "Time heals all wounds; this too shall pass; God doesn't give you more than you can handle".

And these age-old sayings were, as I soon discovered, true. Mark Duran who, with his partner, Ralph Orso, was still owner of a huge salon and spa called Westside, responded to my call by immediately welcoming me to his establishment as a part time employee as well as offering to aid me in any way to make the transition, realizing as he did, that it had been a very long period of time since I worked in a salon environment and that he wanted to ensure my success. He told me that I was one of the best employees he had ever had and that it was his pleasure to have me return to his staff. Furthermore I could start working on Saturdays and Sundays at the salon in January 2004. It was to be the beginning of my glorious journey homeward.

TWENTY-SIX

Ties In The Community

NAOMI, WHO HAD BEEN BUSILY planning the Women's Abuse Center' annual vigil for domestic violence, an event that was, going to take place at the New London County Courthouse outside on the front steps leading into the building, asked me to participate in the ceremony which would be attended by United States senators, attorneys, police administrators, local domestic violence organizations, community officials, religious affiliations, and the administrators of the Women's State Prison in Connecticut, just to name a few. I was honored. And when she asked me to say a few words, I decided to recite a poem, in lieu of a speech, choosing a version of "The Phoenix Bird" which was written by Hans Christian Anderson, a poem that mirrored my life experiences. My introduction which is below is what I read that evening at the Women's Abuse Center' Domestic Violence Vigil which, because of the rain, was held in Rabbi Jacob's temple.

"Welcome. My name is Margo Viola. I am a survivor of domestic violence, and am in awe of this opportunity to give voice to this worthy cause. It is both an honor and a miracle to stand before you today. The Women's Abuse Center was so kind to ask me to participate in this annual vigil, and I hope that my story adds something profound to your life. I speak to you on a topic that touches the core of my being, and I thank all of the individuals who are responsible for my presence here today. The theme of my colloquy could not be expressed or stated without the unwavering support of the Battered Women's Organizations, or the individuals who so selflessly gave to what they so valiantly believe in. For this would not be a reality without their collective effort and relentless fight to reach out, to support and to encourage me and so many other women, a subject addressed by Hans Christian Andersen over a hundred years ago.

'**The Bird of Paradise**—renewed each century—born in flame, ending in flame! Thy picture, in a golden frame, hangs in the halls of the rich, but thou thyself often fliest around, lonely and disregarded, a myth' —"The Phoenix Bird."

The Phoenix Bird, dost thou not know her? She was the woman who did shed blood in the name of love. Who took the blows from the one who vowed to love her. Consumed with guilt, living with the blame for her torture, she tried to make it better. Her remedy was to nurture it, fix it, embrace it and smooth it over. With shattered bone and a broken spirit, she gathered the strength to endure.

The Phoenix Bird, dost thou not know her? She was a mother, a daughter, a sister, a grandmother, an aunt, a friend, a coworker and a neighbor. She was a mother who couldn't shelter her child from the violence inside her own home. She softened her cries, hid her scars and covered her bruises for the safety of her loved ones. She made excuses to protect the one who hurt her. Not to stir more anger, more violence or more pain.

The Phoenix Bird, dost thou not know her? She was a woman blind to her own light, beauty, worth and potential. She was a voiceless shadow who mimicked what was demanded of her. She was the one who wore many masks trying to appease the unappeasable. She was an individual who dare not dream.

The Phoenix Bird, dost thou not know her? She was the one silenced by intimidation. Her inner light faded with isolation. She was there alone imprisoned in a world of torture, fear and contempt. Feeling too alone to reach out, she drowns in a pool of dread.

The Phoenix Bird, dost thou not know her? She is the woman who found the inner strength to crawl up from the darkness and find solace. And with that, she burnt herself into ashes in a funeral pyre. She then rose from the ashes of pain, of suffering, of loneliness and of desperation, to begin her journey toward the healing of her mind, body and spirit. The miracle of life anew is within her. She is radiant in beauty and inner strength. Her essence pulsates through her veins, bringing forth life that is pure and untainted.

The Phoenix Bird, dost thou not know her? She begins her life anew as a challenging adventure one that she cherishes and cultivates. She is shrouded and surrounded by angels. From the ashes of old, springs forth a vital, promising and hopeful life force. It is a life that soars towards the sun of a new dawn. It is filled with warmth, love and a kindred spirit. She is sailing on the wings of life, timeless and filled with limitless potential. She shines as the freshness of a new day.

The Phoenix Bird, dost thou not know her? I do, I am she! The burning of oneself leaves me to call upon my own life story. I remember the darkest corners of my experience, and it allows me to cultivate a new breath of life, one which is undaunted. As the Phoenix Bird burnt the ashes of the old, and regenerated the new, so do I melt down the darkness of my past and create a brilliant rebirth, with the radiance of paradise. From the ugly I melt, I burn, I rise and I renew in beauty.' The Phoenix Bird is not a myth. We all can take this parable and apply it to our lives. There lies a Phoenix Bird in all of us."

It certainly was an evening to remember, one in which I connected with the community at a deeply touching level of awareness. I left the podium with a true feeling of sharing and of giving validity to such an important reality in our society. The growing problem of domestic violence was unveiled that very night in so many creative ways that I was grateful to have taken part in spreading that awareness. It seemed that I was a phoenix bird in real life that I, too, could rise from the ashes of my past.

Twenty-Seven

A New Beginning—Emerged Whole

My journey began the following weekend when I walked into the Westside Salon and Spa not knowing what to expect. Both Mark and Ralph were waiting at the entrance for me, as were the other members of the staff. Even the younger stylist whom I had not known before my incarceration shook my hand and told me it was their pleasure to finally meet me. I felt as though I was finally home and my heart overflowed with gladness.

Marie had been setting up a weekend room for me in the basement of her home. I purchased a bed and a small dresser to accommodate my weekend needs. Marie and Karl would sit on my bed late and night and we would talk about everything in our lives. These were the tender moments we had had to wait a decade to have. My weekends were filled with such precious memories and cherished moments, and Marie, too, seemed to savors these days, able at last to experience the childhood of which she had been so abruptly robbed. Less happily, I noticed that she seemed a bit estranged from her husband which was, perhaps, understandable, given the fact that his mother was living with them, too.

From January to June 2003, I lived two separate lives, in two very different worlds. I still continued my daily work at the legal office Monday through Friday and then on Saturday and Sunday changed into being a mother and a grandmother, as well as a cosmetologist. In these ways, I fulfilled all of my commitments and more, never allowing my insecurities to suffocate my flame for the future which was finally fully realized when, having completed all the parole requirements and paperwork, I was able to rent my new home in Darien which I furnished with consignment furniture. On moving day, Marie, Taylor and I celebrated by ordering pizza which we ate sitting on the floor of my new sanctuary, one that was truly my own.

I was set to begin my full-time position at the salon, both nervous and excited to be living like a normal person, carrying on her daily living activities. It had been a long and difficult road to independence. I hadn't had the time to reflect upon the milestones of accomplishments that I had achieved in that short year. Everyone spoke of them but my deep sense of survival obstructed me from really feeling their impact. However, during the first few days on my own, I felt a tremendous weight lifted off my shoulders and a sense of true deliverance.

I anticipated the new parole supervisor's visit that was to occur at any moment, and was given permission to move into my new place without checking into the district parole office. At that point in time, I had graduated to a three month reporting rotation. I did speak to my new parole officer over the phone but I hadn't met him yet. I was very cautious and skeptical of the entire parole agency. I could never forget the warning I was given about the parole board's outrage at my release. I had been fortunate to have my first parole officer assigned to me but had no idea of who awaited my custody control, at that time.

One evening there was a knock at my door and a man introduced himself to me as Mr. Peter Kenney, Senior Parole Office, a man for whom I had prepared a file listing my achievements since my release from prison. Officer Kenney declared that he was impressed by my new home and told me that, if I needed him for any assistance, he could be reached at the phone numbers on the parole business card. He left after wishing me good luck and saying that he would see me again in three months. My expectations of parole supervision, were so completely opposite of what had just occurred that I was left speechless.

I totally respected every aspect of my freedom, and the guidelines I was bound by, adhering to each one of them, to the letter. I realized my limitations and respected them, but still it was, I knew, necessary to move out of the protective cocoon of Norwich, Connecticut, even though I realized that I could be particularly vulnerable to certain conditions such as that of being surrounded by a crowd, or even seeing a police car, all subtle factors that caused me to become anxious for no good reason except my past experiences.

My outward appearance would sometimes reveal my fear but whenever anyone noticed and asked me if I was okay, I would respond with some humorous comment to avoid an explanation. I was obviously going through psychological and physiological adjustments because I was moving away from my institutionalization. I had spent ten years in a controlled environment, and although I didn't want to admit it, I had been psychologically programed. It would take just as many years to undo the traumatization as it had taken to establish it in the first place, particularly since I was unaware of just how much I had suffered. But since I did know that it would be a long road to recovery and emotional healing, I worked on both my outward physical freedom and inward emotional adjustments.

I found it difficult to communicate my internal fear of the unlocked world around me. One day at work, I was standing in the lunchroom with my coworker when I noticed a delicious desert on top of the counter. I cut a piece of the moist cake and put it in my mouth, and immediately realized that the cake was a holiday rum cake. I spit it in the trashcan, and wash my mouth out with soap because I was petrified that the rum's alcohol was not cooked out and it would cause me to violate my parole. My coworkers were amused by my antics, while I was literally limp with fear of losing my freedom.

Many things that most people took for granted were a blessing to me, and with this in mind, I decided to purchase a puppy to keep me company. And since Marie was convinced that Sara would only welcome another Beagle into her canine circle, we went to a pet shop to find one to match her dog, only to find that the only beagle left was a little fur ball of energy which hung from my pant legs the entire time he was in the pen with us. And since I wasn't ready to tame this wild being, I handed him back to the salesperson and prepared to leave the store disappointed when I noticed this little rust colored puppy which the salesgirl told us was a miniature Dachshund. I asked her to take her out of the cage so that we could take a closer look at her and was thrilled when she immediately cuddled up in my arms, as if to say," I'm yours." From that moment on she was mine forever, a tiny bundle of joy which Marie and I named Mini because she was so tiny. To this day Mini is the queen of my wonderful dachshund brood of four.

During 2004, I had made great stride in my quest for success in my career and family unity. Having been given permission by my parole officer to travel to New York City for several educational classes, I spent an entire weekend in the city that never sleeps, taking a detailed hair extension certification class. With that accreditation, I was able to offer my clients a more expensive custom service which really aided my capacity to grow my business and expand my income. I had a gross intake of over forty thousand dollars that year, and since I had lived very modestly, had been able to save quite a bit of money, my intention being to eventually own a permanent home of my own, a desire that became a necessity when Marie separated from her husband after fourteen months of marriage.

It turned out that Marie and Taylor were not the happy honeymoon couple they should have been. There were a multitude of factors that caused their marriage to dissolve. The communication between them was minimal, and the fact that Taylor's mother, a woman incapable of observing boundaries, was living with them only acerbated the communication barrier between them. Marie loved him, but she allowed her immaturity to control her actions. The manner in which they both conducted their marriage was a recipe for disaster.

I had noticed that Marie had become very close to me after I had a permanent address back home. At first, not wanting to intrude into her relationship with her husband, I thought she was simply enjoying our reunion. But when I realize what was really going on, I tried to advise her to seek professional help with her marriage in regard to the tensions created by living with her mother-in-law. Taylor attempted to appease both Marie and his mother in a non-confrontational manner although it was clear that his marriage wasn't going to continue on his chosen path of least resistance.

When Marie decided to pack her and Karl's belongings and show up at my one bedroom apartment, it was clear that I needed somewhere larger to live in order to accommodate two adults, a child and two dogs. My desire to provide a stable living atmosphere for my family outweighed all of the other priorities in my path, particularly when it was clear that Marie was beginning to regress; the longer we lived in close proximity to one another, the more rapidly she displayed a greater need, both financially and emotionally, for my support. And since Marie had been through a terribly traumatic life experience, I felt a tremendous amount of guilt for her forced path in life. After all, the events that had occurred in my life had directly influenced Marie's, and they happened to her at such an early age that I held myself responsible for her abandonment issues and emotional immaturity. I knew that having me back in her life would come with an enormous amount of healing. And so, with this in mind, I bought a three-bedroom townhouse in the town of Darien, one that was perfect for all of us to live comfortably and happily.

I continued to keep in close contact with Lena and Ted Roma. Lena would visit me at the salon and get her haircut at the same time. It was rumored that Ted, had been nominated to become a Superior Court judge, and I was extremely happy for him and his family, particularly since a judgeship could not have been awarded to a more deserving man. While everyone awaited the governor's signature of approval, I requested to be informed the moment Ted became an official judge. I think that I was as excited for Ted, as he was himself, and was overjoyed when he finally received word that the Connecticut governor had signed him on as a member of the Superior Court. I thought, "Thank the lord that the fruits of Ted' labor had ripened. Let the celebration begin!" Ted's good works and honorable character had been recognized.

His induction was to take place in New London County, Connecticut and I was invited to attend his special ceremony. My answer to Ted's invitation was, "Of course I will be there to see you become a judge, I wouldn't miss it for the world". I was there that evening seated next to Lena Roma, his proud wife, as Ted was sworn into his judge's seat and handed his black robe. The sight brought tears of happiness to my eyes, and my heart filled with such admiration for this man.

The year 2006 was a year to regenerate and renew myself. I had spent three years productively rebuilding my life at a rapid pace, reuniting with my family and cultivating a stable environment, forming a perfect parole status that clearly reflected my deserved freedom, and reconnecting with my daughter on a healing level of renewal in our relationship. I had achieved a host of virtuous accomplishments except to cultivate and transform myself.

And so, with this in mind, I joined a local gym, and convinced Marie to join with me, thinking that sharing an activity such as that would help us reconnect as well as put us in better physical condition, and it was there that I met the godfather of the establishment, Vito Lairdi, a man who knew how to use every piece of equipment that the gym held, as well as how every muscle on the body worked, a five foot six fellow with mocha skin, dark brown hair, and the body of a champion body builder. He was also a man who possessed the sweetest smile and was always ready to help.

As time went by, Vito and I began to see each other more often, and it did not escape my notice that he made a point of speaking to me the moment I walked through the gym doors. His conversations were surprisingly articulate as opposed to that of most of the muscle heads in the gym. Usually men with his physical appearance had a three-word vocabulary at best, but Vito was intelligent, well rounded and had a vast vocabulary. Not only did we share similar backgrounds and beliefs, but also he was gentle, calm and kind with a soulful look in his eyes which I found enormously appealing. He spoke of the women in his life, particularly his deceased mother, with great respect and pride. And he was ambitious, determined to secure a body building title. We both decided to meet at the gym partnering together, to aid each other in our weight training.

I was certainly attracted to the man, and it did not hurt that Marie respected Vito and thought he would be a good match for me. First and foremost, we began a friendship. I was not interested in a romantic relationship, and Vito respected my wishes, although he kept patiently and secretly courting me, assuring me that, when he asked me out for coffee, it was not a date.

Before long, we were in a relationship and I was completely satisfied with this new avenue of freedom as I slowly allowed myself to feel for man again. It was a sublime new existence for me. But the deeper our relationship grew, the more nervous I began to be that it would end, particularly when we reached the point when it was clear it was only fair to tell Vito where my life's path had taken me. And although Marie was confident that Vito would accept everything about me including my imprisonment, I was not so sure about what his reaction would be.

One evening, ready at last to share my past history with him, I invited Vito over to my house for dinner, fully aware that, after he had heard my story, there was a good chance he would head for the nearest door. However, we had reached a fork in the road. I had to take that roll of the dice, because I couldn't go on another day withholding the truth from him.

It took me until after dinner when we were sitting on the couch together to bolster my courage sufficiently to be completely frank. "What I am about to tell you, I am not obligated to divulge to you or anyone," I began. "I want you to sit and listen closely to what I am going to share with you. It's difficult for me to find the words to explain everything, but I want you to know that I have grown to trust you completely. Our relationship has grown faster and deeper than I ever imagined it to be. I care for you deeply and I want you to realize that my past does not define or equal who I am! In fact, my past has helped me to become the person I am today. When I am finished telling you what I need to get off my mind, I will fully understand if you terminate our relationship."

And with that I went on to tell him that I was the woman from Darien who, thirteen years earlier, had been arrested and charged with the death of my abusive boyfriend. I told him that I had spent ten years in prison, and had been released three years ago and was on parole, which would last another two years before I would complete my full sentence.

Vito was clearly overwhelmed with amazement. "I thought you looked familiar but I didn't put two and two together," he told me. "In fact, I vividly remember the day you were arrested. I thought then that you had had a really raw deal and now that I know the facts, I am so sorry that this happened to you. But in a strange way, I'm relieved, because I thought that you were going to say that you were breaking up with me."

After that response, I knew Vito was the man for me. He was so sweet and so unaffected by my past which he said was over and gone, something I never had to think about if I choose not to, and went on to urge me to focus, as he intended to do, on our new life together, not on past history. Vito was truly amazing man.

As our relationship continued to grow deeper, we decided to compete together in an annual bodybuilding contest, and toward that end worked diligently each day on our diet, weight lifting routine, posing exercises and personal ninety-second muscle presentation, sculpting our physical appearance and sharing criticism. I had more energy and stage presence of the sort that would attract the judge's attention, and he helped me lose my inclination to assume stiff poses. We were a true dream team.

Our efforts paid off in the most exciting way imaginable. The bodybuilding completion was held at the local community college. Our family members and coworkers came and showed their support by whistling and hooting on our behalf as I placed first in the Master's Division and second in the Open Division while Vito took second place in the Master's Division and third in the Open Division. After the ceremonies ended, we took our families out for a big dinner to celebrate our victory.

There was so much to be thankful for. My daughter was in a steady relationship with a guy she cared for greatly, settling down at last from her long wild run in the single jungle, finally able to recognize the fact that there really wasn't anything special out in the world that she had missed. Like me, she learned to be grateful for all that we had and to build on it for a better future.

The year 2007 was filled with dramatic changes in all aspects of my life. The economy had taken a nosedive all over the United States and the housing market was on a downslide, which eventually almost caused the stock market to crash. With people running scared, spending almost came to a halt. Government predictions showed that the economy was about to become worse not better. And on top of all this, the township where I resided was conducting property reappraisals which meant my taxes were about to increase significantly. As a consequence, people were not concerned with luxury spending because many of them were being laid off from their jobs; even my puppy business was facing hard times. I was worried that I would not be able to afford the upkeep of my financial obligations.

At the same time, since Vito and I were in love, and our relationship flourishing, he moved into my house to help me pay the bills, and shortly afterwards proposed to me, saying, as he offered me the ring, that he had waited his entire lifetime to find true love, "I've had three true loves in my life and they were my mother, my daughter and now you," he said. "Will you marry me?"

We planned to get married in one year when I had completed parole. In between that time, we evaluated our goals as future husband and wife, and decided that we should sell my house and move into our own home together. My daughter was, of course, glad for me, and realized that it was time that our living arrangement ended. She was in her own relationship and hoped to settle down herself. It was part of the natural cycle of life for her to leave the nest and move on to adulthood. I promised to get her started in a home of her own.

I put my house on the market in May 2007 without a realtor and sold it within two weeks to a divorced woman with three teenage daughters who was downsizing and who fell in love with my home and all the improvements I had made. After searching desperately for a new property to purchase in Fairfield County, Vito and I found a perfect little house located in Darien. I was a bit apprehensive because I would have to be assigned to a different parole officer, but we decided to buy it spite of any parole complications which, as it turned out, presented no problems. We purchased the house that suited both our lifestyle and financial means. I only had a year left to serve out my entire sentence so we went along with the temporary inconvenience.

I was assigned to an Officer Green, a complete professional who took her job very seriously. Over the year she conducted unannounced home visits so often that Vito and I joked that she must be planning to move in, and soon became a friend who clearly appreciated our openness and honesty. On June 25, 2008, I officially became a free woman.

On June 27, 2008, our marriage ceremony took place. I had wanted Ted Roma to marry us since, by that time, he was a Superior Court judge and had been vested with the power to perform the marriage ceremony. It was so meaningful for Ted to be the person who joined Vito and I together.

Our intention to have a simple ceremony at Ted's house was changed when my co-workers and friends, many of whom had known me for my entire lifetime, announced that they wanted to be part of the proceedings, with the result that my boss insisted that we be married at his salon, an eight thousand square feet, two floor establishment, elegantly furnished with a double staircase presided over by a huge crystal chandelier.

Everyone extended suggestions and volunteered to participate in making our wedding day really special. Some decorated, while others volunteered to bring specialty foods, including tea sandwiches, while my old friend Sonny ordered a wedding cake as his gift to us, and I managed to find three high school music students that came to play the violin and cello. Everyone chipped in and set up the salon for a beautiful celebration.

Ted, now referred to as Judge Roma, brought his family with him to take part in our day, the highlight of which was, of course, the ceremony which took place on the landing of the double staircase with my daughter and grandson standing to our left and Vito's daughter and two sons to the right while all of our guests looked down at us from the upper level. Judge Ted spoke so eloquently of his happiness for our new beginning. It was the most meaningful wedding that I could have dreamed of.

"I hope to find a man someday just like you, Vito," Marie said in her toast, "a man that will love me, as much as, you love my mom. Mom you deserve this happiness and much more. I love you both so much."

Love and the people who really mattered surrounded us in our celebration. They all bore witness to our loving new beginning, starting with a honeymoon in a penthouse suite of a cruise ship sailing to the Caribbean. As I looked back on my life, a journey filled with powerful lessons, I have, I find, no resentment, no shame. Instead I am ready to embrace all the experiences that life brings to me. I am certain, that my life was meant to teach lessons to others, as well as to myself. I have to believe that because, otherwise, all that I have suffered and all that I have learned would be for naught.

"To life"

Lightning Source UK Ltd.
Milton Keynes UK
UKOW05f1819030115

243931UK00001B/252/P